Cricket Skills and Techniques

Cricket Skills and Techniques

A comprehensive guide to coaching and playing

Doug Wright
With a foreword by Colin Cowdrey

Arthur Barker Limited
5 Winsley Street London W1

ISBN 0 213 00464 x

Printed in Great Britain by
Bristol Typesetting Co Ltd Barton Manor Bristol

Contents

Acknowledgements

I am deeply indebted to John Fogg of *The Daily Telegraph*, without whose technical skill, professional advice – and patience – this book might never have been written. I am also grateful to George Craig for the excellent line drawings which illustrate the coaching points.

Illustrations

Foreword

'Now then, Sir Donald, who was the greatest bowler you batted against?' Predictably, if you know the Bradman sense of humour, he replied: 'I don't remember any!' I pressed him further, for I value his judgement.

Upon reflection, he spoke highly of Maurice Tate and Bill O'Reilly, and with understandable feeling of the terrifying pace and accuracy of Harold Larwood. Ian Peebles' googly was very hard to spot and clearly Alec Bedser and Ray Lindwall were truly great.

Then his eyes lit up. 'There was one who caused me more problems than anyone else – Douglas Wright of Kent. He was at times erratic, expensive and could be a real headache for the fielding captain defending a small score. I scored a lot of runs against him,' he went on, 'yet I could never settle down comfortably. However well set I was and on the best batting wickets, I knew that he was capable of producing the unplayable ball – and no other bowler had quite the same power.' This was praise indeed.

What a sight Douglas Wright was on his long run at a new batsman, even on a good wicket (and his record of seven hat tricks is proof of this) with a slip and a gully, four short legs and the inimitable Godfrey Evans behind the wicket in support. As a Kent schoolboy sitting on the grass and too shy to ask for an autograph, this was my area of hero worship and my idea of heaven.

Imagine my excitement when at length I play my first match for Kent and then my anxiety as a high, swirling, spinning catch plummets towards me off the great man's bowling. Somehow I clung on and, while I was waiting to see whether my heart would start beating again, my hero was approaching. 'Well done, young fellah! Anyone who takes catches for me becomes a friend for life.' Happily, over the years, this has come to be.

First and foremost, Douglas was a kind, generous person, never given to glaring at batsmen or chiding his fielders. He was the unluckiest bowler in the world and he suffered more than anyone with near misses. At the same time, he was a very tough competitor who relished the tussle with a great batsman. Wright versus Compton at Lord's and Canterbury were rare feasts of cricket entertainment. He was at his best on the big occasion when the wicket was all in favour of the batsman.

Second, he was a perfectionist. He adored practice and experiment. In this respect he was a magnificent example to his colleagues and a spur to the conscience of the lazy. There can never have been a more whole-hearted trier.

Third, behind a shy and reserved exterior lay a deceptively adroit cricket brain. He analysed batsmen well and knew exactly how he was going to bowl to each. This splendid book reveals just how deeply he thought about the game and I have enjoyed his bowler's views on the art of batsmanship.

I count it a privilege to have played with Douglas Wright, a magnificent bowler and a true gentleman with a passionate love of the game. I commend this book to both young and old, to those who teach and those who learn, and I am delighted to have the first word in it.

Colin Cowdrey

1

Developing Ability

The 'skill and technique of cricket' has always been of great interest to me. I started my cricketing career at the Faulkner School of Cricket in 1930, under that fine coach Major G. A. Faulkner, the South African leg-break bowler. At his school I met all types of cricketers, from international and county players to the youngest schoolboy, all coming to seek his advice. I was engaged in the office and I had a promise from the 'Major' that I could occasionally bowl in the nets. The normal conversation in the school was cricket technique and everything connected with cricket was thoroughly expounded, disagreed with, argued about and finally settled by the Major, whose opinions were accepted unquestionably.

The Major kept his promise; I bowled at the nets and it was then that I began to appreciate the skill and technique of cricket. After bowling a few balls at a player, I realized that here was someone of some ability, or perhaps that a batsman had this or that fault. This early training at the nets helped me tremendously to size up the batsmen during my twenty-five years of county cricket and, what is so important now, to notice quickly any faults in young players.

Sometimes I was allowed to have a knock in the nets and it was then that I found that although technique is very necessary, in fact vital to everyone, one could only be as good as one's natural ability would allow. I do not intend to try to explain the meaning of 'natural ability' but I am willing to accept the fact that some batsmen are able to see the ball very quickly and appear to know immediately which way to move and do so easily in the correct manner, this correct manner being the

' technique' which is not a natural method but one that can be taught to almost anyone.

In later years, when I joined the Kent staff, I always marvelled at the ease with which Arthur Fagg, Kent's opening batsman and now a leading Test umpire, could see, move into position, hook even the fastest bowler – yet, *without the ball* I could play the shot as well as Arthur. I had the technique, but not enough skill.

During my time at the cricket school I watched the Major bowl leg-breaks and googlies, I even had the great pleasure of batting to him, and I remember quite clearly his chuckle when I didn't see the googly and was caught with legs in front of the wicket. There seemed to be only one type of bowling worth thinking about and I suppose I was particularly lucky in being able to spin the ball, without even imagining that it was difficult or unusual to do so. I cannot remember being told how to hold the ball or what to do, but I must admit that I found great difficulty in pitching it consistently where I wanted, and this has remained a constant worry throughout my career.

The technique of cricket changed very little during my playing years. Although several players used their own particular method and style, the basic shots were still played in the same manner. Denis Compton had his sweep to leg which, played as he did to a ball pitching just outside the leg stump and reaching out to play on the half volley, was in fact a fairly sound shot. I do disagree most emphatically with people who say that Denis was unorthodox. He did play one or two quite delightful shots that one would not suggest to a young cricketer; these were shots of someone in the very top category. However, when it was necessary for him to play defensively either forward or back, he then produced a shot technically perfect and superbly timed. Even Sir Donald Bradman has not escaped the critics. It has been said that he was uncoached and unorthodox. The tremendous success that Sir Don had was not made by unorthodox methods, but by a very sound technique and tremendous application.

There are slight changes in batting techniques according to the state of the wicket. One of the most noticeable differences in the method of some overseas players is that they are more ready to square cut anything that is slightly short and near the off stump. The fast and true pitches of the West Indies give a consistent bounce and little deviation, and the batsman can even 'give himself room' if the ball is on the short side. Yet again, when the ball is pitched fairly well up and comes on to the bat quickly, it can be driven with more confidence. The pitches in England pre-war, and up until almost 1950, were generally fairly quick and true and they were conducive to shot-making. The bowler had to make the ball do something, and not rely on the wicket to help him, and the batsman was thinking in terms of scoring runs, rather than waiting for the bad ball.

During the last fifteen years the pitches have not improved. In fact, they seem to have lost pace and, in quite a few instances, have been just plain bad wickets. The batsman of today appears to be rather afraid to commit himself to a forward shot, in case the ball does something unusual, and therefore he sometimes plays forward with the bat 'behind his front leg'. This technique of playing on today's pitches is not one that I like, or in fact agree with. I am particularly distressed to find that many young boys whom I meet at schools have been coached in this way. One must not 'lunge forward' to a ball pitching short of a length – particularly when it is turning sharply – and push the bat out at arm's length, as it is obvious one cannot get near the pitch. In this case, if one is forward, perhaps it is best to wait and play close to the front foot. However, as the mistake was to go *forward* at all to this delivery, a forcing *back* shot might have been played.

I intend to explain the forward and back shots (the basic shots) in full detail later on, as complete mastery and understanding of these shots is absolutely essential. One must realize that either the batsman plays forward (and this means getting to, or as near as possible to, the pitch of the ball) or if the ball pitches short – the batsman plays back. I can find only one

B

saving grace on playing forward with bat behind pad. That is
when an off-spinner is turning the ball sharply on a bad wicket
and the batsman is not too happy about his ability to ' cover
the ball ' at its pitch. For the young cricketer to be taught to
play in this method is courting disaster and, as I know from
considerable experience, several boys have found it extremely
difficult to correct. This new method of playing forward has
worried me for several years, and when I was approached to
write this book on ' Skills and Techniques ' I immediately
jumped at the chance.

When one is a bowler, earning one's living by playing county
cricket, the main preoccupation is not only bowling the ball but
also judging the batting technique of the batsman whom you
are opposing. I suppose that even now I have a fairly clear
picture of most of the leading players' strong points and where
I considered was the best place to attack the batsman. I also
still have a mental note of those players who could pick the
' wrong 'un ', and of those who were not too sure. After a few
years, one could almost tell from the stance and the pick-up
just how good a player was. Let me say very quickly that I do
not suggest I had the measure of all these players, but that
simply by watching their method of playing I had perhaps a
little more chance of getting their wicket. However, I had to
pitch the ball in the correct spot and this was not at all easy.
This experience of watching closely most of the world's best
batsmen is an answer to those who wonder why a bowler should
feel so strongly about batting techniques.

Bowling does have a technique and there are many ways of
improving a young bowler. Perhaps a bowler relies more on his
natural ability, but it is surprising how little is really understood
by the average cricketer about bowling.

Is coaching really necessary? Do we have too much coaching?
We hear these questions asked almost daily. I think the answer
to the first question is yes – coaching is necessary, especially for
the young. We also do not have too much *good* coaching, for
I am sorry to say that there is a certain amount of coaching

that does more harm than good. Let me give an example. I was coaching a boy at a preparatory school to bowl orthodox left-arm spinners and he was bowling them quite well. The master in charge of cricket, who had been watching at the batting end, came along and questioned the boy on what he was bowling. When the boy replied, 'Spinners, sir,' his only remark was ' Well, make sure you swing the ball in as well.' Another favourite remark is, ' Use your feet ', given to some poor little boy who hardly knows how to hold the bat.

Coaching can be obtained in several ways. The obvious way, of course, is to employ a coach for three or four boys in a net for an hour. Probably the best way, particularly for a beginner, is to have individual coaching for the first lesson at least. There are people who say that they have never had any coaching in their life. When one enquires as to how they started playing, one generally finds that they have spent many hours watching first-class cricket. This is what I call ' indirect coaching', and if one has sufficient ability and perseverance this may be all that is necessary. Leslie Ames of Kent is one man who had no coaching, but admits to spending many hours watching at the county grounds. I think it is obvious that some coaching is necessary. The greatest players have needed very little coaching, yet there are a few who by sheer hard work have made the grade, even in Test cricket. Most people do not make the best of their ability for various reasons, generally because they are not able to apply themselves sufficiently. A coach's job is to make the most of a pupil's natural ability. This includes taking into account the player's age, character, temperament and powers of concentration and application. How frustrating coaching can be when one realizes how many permutations there are to get enough of the correct ingredients together to make a first-class player.

A lot has been said for and against group coaching. I am very much in favour, as I consider that it saves so much time for both pupil and coach. If a boy cannot play both basic shots – that is, the forward and back defensive shots – without a ball, he certainly will not be able to do so with a ball. However tedious it may be at first for a pupil to practise shots without a ball, eventually it will pay handsome dividends. After the player has become proficient without a ball, a tennis ball can be used, thrown from a short distance at first. The next step is to go into the nets and use a hard ball. Even at this stage it is best for the coach to take the pupil alone for the initial net. Once the two basic shots have been mastered, other shots will follow automatically.

At what age should one start to coach a boy? This must depend on the individual; some boys can concentrate and have enough ability to start at even eight years of age, but the average age is about ten. Great care must be taken not to bore the young player, although one must implant correct methods as soon as possible. Cricket is a very demanding game needing correct technique if one is going to reach any standard. It is therefore very essential that boys should not be allowed to make many incorrect shots, as these will be very difficult to eradicate later on. As I have said, care must be taken to keep the pupil's interest, yet one must coax and continually strive for perfection and do this gradually without appearing to be too strict. Nothing is more harmful than allowing a young boy just to hit the ball aimlessly. Discipline in batting is just as necessary for the beginner as for the Test player.

Many people do not realize fully the importance of the pitch, whether it be for a Test match or for net practice for the youngest pupil. Far too many young boys are coached on poor wickets; in fact they are expected to play most of their cricket on pitches completely unsuitable and often dangerous. One of the greatest drawbacks to cricket at the moment, whether it be Test match, county match or just a game on the local recreation ground, is the lack of first-class pitches. It is very frustrating for the coach to see boys who have been coached on a good pitch playing their matches on poor wickets and being caught off the glove or bowled by a ' shooter '. One cannot play cricket on a bad pitch and not even on a fairly good one – it must be in first-class condition. The late Sid Barnes, who was a great Test-match bowler, once said you cannot make a bowler by giving him a bad pitch. You will not make a batsman either!

Before entering upon a more detailed examination of the techniques, perhaps I ought to ensure that all pupils have given thought to their equipment: that trousers are not too tight, that boots are spiked and that pads fit; also that the necessary abdominal protection is worn. May I make a plea to the fathers who allow their small sons to use their bats – please buy the boy his own bat, making sure he gets the correct size, even if it is a cheap or second-hand one. However much the boy says he likes your bat, it will not benefit his cricket and will probably cause a lot of harm in the future.

During Easter coaching classes at Canterbury, I was waiting in the dressing-room for the boys to arrive when I noticed in a corner a cricket bat that looked rather interesting. When I picked it up, or at least tried to, I was astounded at its weight, and on further study found that the rubber on the handle had perished and was quite hard. This full-size bat was highly polished and the colour of mahogany but what amazed me most was its enormous thickness and obvious age. It was hard to believe that any boy could possibly use the bat, as I found difficulty in making a shot with it. When the boys arrived I found to my horror that the bat belonged to the smallest boy in the class. 'Are you going to use that bat?' I asked, and he replied, 'Yes, sir, it belonged to my grandfather and it's got a lovely drive.' I am sorry to say I did not convince the boy that it was not the bat for him. I only hope it broke, but I doubt it.

I am continually being surprised by the enormous amount of care and attention that some people lavish on a new bat. They purposefully go to the shop and pick out their bat at least six months before the start of the season. They then oil it – carefully missing the splice – two or three times, after which they either use an old ball, or a specially made mallet, and tap, tap away at the face until they fancy the bat is fully broken in and ready for use. But I have also seen a brand new bat, unoiled and straight from the factory taken out and used successfully in a county match. I am still wondering if the batsman noticed the difference! Here are my suggestions for any of you buying a new bat this year. Choose a bat that ' picks up ' easily and without effort. Make a few imaginary shots with it to see if you like the weight and balance. Don't count the grains or worry over any slight redness – this is often a good sign. When satisfied oil it once all over – yes, splice and back as well. When dry, tap with an old ball to see if you can get a nice ' buttery' bounce; if so, then no more than two light coatings of oil – faces and edges only – will be necessary. If the bat sounds a little hard, another coating of oil and more tapping will soon loosen the hardness.

When your bat is dirty, clean with fine sandpaper and then a very, very light oiling. Clean, oil and store away in winter well clear of any excessive heat.

2
Batting Basics

We may assume that the batsman has got to the wicket correctly padded and equipped. He now has to take guard; this means that by holding his bat in an upright position on the pitch he is guided by the umpire at the bowling end to line his bat up with any of the stumps he chooses. The normal guard taken is middle-and-leg stump. A small mark is made by the batsman on the popping crease and he now knows where he is standing in relation to the wicket.

When the bowler runs to the wicket and delivers the ball, there are four things the batsman has to do. He must watch the ball, decide which shot to play and then make the shot. Watching the ball is not easy; it takes a lot of concentration although some batsmen appear to find it much easier than others. To decide correctly which stroke to play is a natural instinct which may be improved by practice, up to a certain standard. Making the shot correctly is the least difficult thing to do. I am sure that most people, if they are not physically handicapped, can with practice make all cricket shots – without a ball – reasonably well. Lastly we have to co-ordinate and make the shot at the correct time. This is the revealing test of one's ability.

Good batting depends on playing straight and to do this one must keep the body sideways. For a right-handed batsman the dominant hand is the left hand, the right hand being used mostly for applying power. I should perhaps emphasize at this stage that the following advice is based on a right-handed batsman; left-handers should reverse the positions.

The Grip

To try to change the grip of someone who has even a little success at batting is inadvisable and often disastrous. For the young cricketer there is a grip which I am sure in most cases gives the best result. The hands are held close together, not overlapping, half-way up the handle of the bat. The fingers and thumbs are held round the handle. On no account must a finger be put straight down the handle or it will be badly injured if hit by the ball. Hold the bat very firmly with the left hand and keep the back of the hand pointing in the direction between midoff and extra cover when the bat is held upright. The right hand need not be held too tightly, because in the forward and back defensive shots the fingers have to loosen to allow the bat to be held at the correct angle. Finally the vs formed by the thumbs and forefingers should be in line with each other.

I advise any young player to use this grip as it will help in keeping the face of the bat to the ball on all the straight bat

Figure 1 Grip and stance

shots. I am well aware that many batsmen have not used this grip and yet have succeeded, but this is in spite of their grip, and not because of it.

Stance

I feel very much the same way about the stance as the grip. There is a stance which I am sure will give best results but you should not think of changing if you have been trained for any length of time and have been fairly successful with an alternative. The feet should be placed parallel to the popping crease, one foot on each side of the line about six inches apart. Care must be taken to see the back foot is *behind* the crease. The weight should be evenly balanced and knees slightly relaxed for quick movement. The left shoulder should point at the bowler. The head should be upright and turned fully on, so that both eyes are level. The bat gripped in the correct manner is placed close to the legs, the bottom of the bat just touching the outside of the right toe and the hands resting on the left thigh. The batsman should be completely balanced and able to see without difficulty both sides of the pitch, as well as move quickly either forward or backward. Some batsmen need to open their stance slightly for greater freedom on the leg side, but any large alteration can cause trouble.

Back Lift

With eyes glued on the ball in the bowler's hand, the batsman's first movement is to pick the bat up as the bowler's arm is coming over to deliver the ball. Keeping head and body still, he pushes the bat straight back in line with the middle stump by the left arm bending at the elbow and keeping the right arm fairly close to the side. The face of the bat will open towards point. Do not pick the bat up too high until you are sure of the shot you have to play. If it is a bad ball you will then have time to pick the bat up a little higher. With practice you will find that the bat will be picked up according to the ball to be played.

Figure 2 Back lift

Care must be taken, however, not to get into the habit of picking the bat up too high, as it is very vulnerable to the faster ball. It is also much more difficult to bring it down straight.

I must admit that many great players have not picked their bats up straight. Such players of my day as Sir Don Bradman and Keith Miller both held the bat between their feet, whence it was quite impossible to pick their bat up straight. What was far more important was that they brought the bat *down* straight. If the right elbow is kept fairly close to the body on the pick-up it will help the left hand bring the bat down on a straight line. From all that has been said it must be obvious that to pick the bat up straight is a very good beginning to a stroke that *must* have the bat brought down straight.

A very good method of practising the pick-up is to take your stance as close as possible to a wall and then pick the bat up without the bat touching the wall. Another very useful practice

Figure 3 Practising back lift

is to play shots in front of a full length mirror. Practise until you can make all shots automatically; you will then be able to give all your attention to the ball.

Forward Defensive Shot

Having picked our bat up straight, and watching the ball carefully, we are now ready to play our first shot. The ball is of medium pace pitching on a length and we must therefore play a forward defensive shot. The left shoulder is pushed out to a position that you consider the ball will pitch; at the same time the bent left leg is placed as close to the line the ball will take allowing just enough room for the bat to come through. If the left shoulder is pushed out and is kept over the left knee, the batsman cannot overreach. The ball is played in front of the left leg and as close as possible to the pitch with the bat at an

Figure 4 Forward defensive stroke

angle slightly inclined to the ground. The head is behind and over the bat and the majority of weight is now on the left foot. The right foot *must* have some part of it on the ground behind the line. The heel of the right foot must never be allowed to turn over and point to the off side, as this will allow the shoulders to turn and may cause the bat to come off line. When placing the left foot forward do not point it at the ball but allow it to fall naturally and the toes will now be pointing to extra cover. The bat is brought through to the ball by the left hand and arm just after the body is balanced on the left foot, and the right hand grip must now be adjusted to a finger-tip hold to allow the bat to slope at the correct angle.

An interesting exercise is to draw a line from the middle stump straight down the pitch and then practise making the pick-up and forward defensive shot on the line. It is very revealing to see the actual path of the bat down the line.

Many boys whom I have had to coach have been wrongly informed about the left foot and playing forward. They think

Figure 5 Forward defensive stroke

that unless they can get their left foot to where the ball actually pitches, they should not go forward. This causes the boy to stretch out much too far, and in consequence he throws his body backwards with dire results. If you are playing a forward defensive shot you must leave the face of the bat to the ball and *not* carry on with the shot.

I have noticed that in the last few years there has been a tendency, especially among the younger players, to make the angle of the bat on both the forward and back defensive shots much more acute. To increase the angle of the bat when the ball is moving a lot is one method of keeping the ball down, but this can be overdone, particularly on good wickets.

The forward defensive stroke is a basic shot, a foundation on which all other forward straight-bat shots are played. Although I

have explained how to play forward to a ball that pitches
straight, the execution to a ball pitching either on the off or leg
side is virtually the same. I have yet to meet a first-class player
who could not play this shot satisfactorily when necessary.

A quick recap, for the young enthusiast. Make sure your
stance is correct – feet, knees, hips and shoulders sideways on to
bowler. Head well round and looking over left shoulder at ball.
Top hand grip facing extra cover, pick-up behind you and bring
bat down straight. Left shoulder to pitch over bent left knee,
right foot on toes but grounded behind line. Firm left hand and
trap ball at pitch with slightly angled bat; *leave* face of bat to
ball. Practise this without the ball, and also in front of a mirror.
Play shot on the white line slowly at first, and then quicken up
and get a friend to keep an eye on the path of your bat. Practise
pick-up and forward shot with left hand only.

Back Defensive Shot

The alternative to the forward defensive shot is the back
defensive. This shot is played to a ball pitching on a length, but
not quite so far up as to allow the batsman to deal with it
safely forward at its pitch. In this case one steps back, giving
a little more time to see the ball off the pitch and enabling one to
play more easily. The first movement is back with the right
foot, placing it approximately half-way to the stumps and
behind the spot on which the ball pitched. All the weight is taken
on the back foot, the front foot just touching the ground to
keep one's balance. The body is tilted slightly forward over the
right leg which is placed parallel to the popping crease. With a
firm left wrist and left elbow upright, the bat is brought through
just past the right leg. The bat should be slightly inclined to the
ground when it meets the ball. The right-hand grip loosens to
finger-tip grip, similar to the right hand in the forward shot.
The main points to watch are: to step back behind the pitch of
the ball, providing the ball pitches in line with the wickets; if
the ball pitches outside the off stump the right foot should cover

Figure 6 Back defensive stroke

the off stump and go no farther; when the ball pitches outside the leg stump, the right foot steps back into the wicket turning the body to allow the face of the bat to meet the ball.

Do not push out at the ball; let it come to you. Providing you have moved behind the pitch, you are now in the best position to play the ball even if it moves after pitching in, or away, from you. Like all cricket shots the ball must be played at the correct time, and as this is a defensive shot the face of the bat must be left at the ball.

Many cricketers appear to scorn the idea of finishing either defensive shot correctly and then wonder why they get out. These two shots must be practised to perfection and you will then find you are in the correct position to play most of the actual scoring shots.

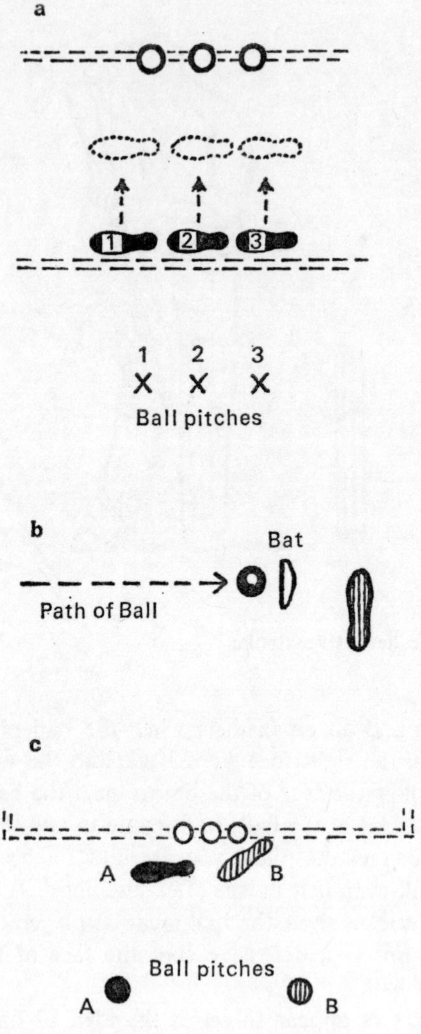

a

1 2 3
X X X
Ball pitches

b

Bat

Path of Ball

c

A   B

Ball pitches
A   B

Figure 7a Position of right foot when ball comes straight through
Figure 7b Right foot almost in line with ball
Figure 7c Position of right foot to A ball pitching outside off stump
          B ball pitching outside leg stump

3

Batting for Runs

The pattern of the game is now unfolding. We now know that if the ball pitches up we have to play forward to meet it, and that if it is short we must go back making it even shorter. We can now play a forward and back defensive shot and this at least will allow us to stay at the wicket. Unfortunately we cannot get many runs this way and therefore must now consider the scoring shots.

Forward Straight Drive

Firstly let us learn to play a straight drive off the front foot. This shot is played to a ball that pitches straight and is far enough up to let us get our left foot to the pitch. This half-volley is hit as it bounces, and the ball will then keep to the ground. The technique for this shot is relatively easy now that you can play the forward defensive. The left shoulder is over the left knee and the left foot is placed just beside the spot the ball has pitched. The left arm guides the face of the bat to the ball and the right hand with full grip produces the power to drive the ball as it pitches. The bat then follows through and in this case should point straight down the wicket. In the case of the ball pitching outside the off stump the bat should go straight through following the direction of the ball. There are two methods of finishing the drive: one is to pronate the wrists and the other is to keep the face of the bat to the ball.

The first method of turning the wrists over does give a more rhythmic flow to the shot, but care must be taken not to twist the wrists too early. The second method is perhaps better for

Figure 8 Forward straight drive

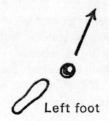

Left foot

Right foot

Figure 9 Forward drive

the younger player, as it ensures the face of the bat meeting the ball. However, with this method care must be taken to keep the head down. Most county players favour the first method, but Colin Cowdrey likes the second and he, of course, is noted for his fine driving. All forward drives are played in the same manner although some batsmen dip the left shoulder and point the left toe to the ball for on drives. This does help to get the head over the ball.

There is a tendency among young batsmen to think that any ball pitching up near the off stump must be played past cover, and they allow their right foot to move round to enable them to do this. Each ball must be played according to where it pitches, and if it pitches straight then it should be hit straight back past the bowler. Another fallacy is suggesting to the young batsman to play the ball through the gap, or to the left or right hand of the fielder. Most of this talk is utter nonsense; to play the ball straight and to keep it on the ground is more than enough for most boys. Good advice for straight driving is to ' throw your hands through the ball '.

Figure 10 Forward straight drive

Figure 11 Forward straight drive

One word of warning before off driving: beware of the wily slow bowler who gets you playing forward and gradually bowls wider and wider. Remember the ball must pitch up a little farther according to the width.

For sheer perfection of the off drive I have never seen any one to equal Wally Hammond. He had a majestic stance, great power and grace and perfect technique producing superb cover drives which skimmed to the boundary. These shots gained four runs for the batsman and immense pleasure for the spectators. At the time of writing I have not had the pleasure of watching the skill and driving power of the young South African Barry Richards who also plays for Hampshire. From reports of his prowess in the 1970-1 Australian season he may

Figure 12 Forward straight drive

well be in the Hammond class. Of contemporary left-handers Graeme Pollock and Gary Sobers – inevitably – play off drives with grace and force.

A choice remark from a young pupil who was satisfactorily playing both defensive shots rather shook me. 'Mr Wright,' he said, 'how do you *play* the unplayable ball?'

'Use Your Feet'

I have already mentioned that the phrase 'use your feet' is too often quoted to the inexperienced. I have even heard a coach suggest that the pupil should take one pace down the wicket to deal with a good-length ball. This is of course ridiculous. For the young boy who is learning the game and struggling to play even the basic shots correctly, it is asking too much to expect

Figure 13 Moving out to drive

him to charge down the wicket, even if he knows how. I am quite aware that the ball should be hit, but there is a correct method that must be employed if any consistency is to be hoped for. It is possible that in the one-day cricket matches of today some players may use their feet to slow and fast bowlers, but this is a necessity caused by the limit of overs. When a boy gets to an advanced stage he can then be shown how to move down the wicket, but this is not at all essential for all batsmen. There have been many fine players who have not danced down the pitch, or at least only very occasionally.

It is not the be-all-and-end-all of batsmanship, although I must admit that if someone possesses the ability to do it successfully, it is very upsetting to the bowler. However, it is a very dangerous shot, and needs a lot of practice which you can get only in the nets. A batsman who is slow on his feet would do better to stay at home in his crease and concentrate on those

Figure 14 Moving out to drive

shots he is capable of playing, and leave chasing the ball to the quick-footed player. The main thing about moving down the wicket is to keep one's head steady and watch the ball. To do this one must *glide* out. The left foot takes a full pace, the right foot sliding up behind it in a chassé movement, and finally the left leg is placed to the pitch of the ball in exactly the same manner as with a forward drive. The length of each stride will depend on the distance a batsman has to go to get to the pitch – the whole movement must be as smooth as possible. It must be remembered that once the batsman has left the crease he *must* get to the pitch.

Whenever I have bowled to a batsman who has moved down the pitch, and then has decided he is not quite to the ball, and has played a defensive shot, I am sure that here is a very good player. So many people rush down the pitch with the one intention of hitting the ball out of sight, and then pay the penalty.

During Canterbury Cricket Week just before the war, a Somerset batsman named Case was batting against Tich Freeman. On three successive balls he walked down the pitch and hit them straight over the stand for six. The fourth ball he missed and he was so far down the wicket that he just continued walking to the pavilion.

'Use your feet' is a very stupid remark to make to anyone but the most advanced player. Even he will need a lot of practice in the nets, and in the middle, before using it in a serious match. '*Use your foot*' (be it left or right) is a remark I would be very pleased to hear much more often.

The Lofted Drive

Another straight bat shot off the front foot is the straight drive for six, or intentionally hitting over mid off and mid on. As I have mentioned elsewhere, the pace of the pitch and the speed of the bowler determine to some extent the technique one has to use.

The ideal ball to hit for six is one that lands on a length on a fairly quick pitch from a bowler of medium pace. The normal technique for the straight drive can be used and no extra effort made to lift the ball, because from a good length it will be rising as it meets the bat. May I emphasize once again that all forward shots played with a straight bat are played in the same manner? Left shoulder and left foot to the pitch and right foot kept in the same position as a stance, but now grounded only by the toe. The right foot is most important, and it cannot be over-stressed that if the right foot is allowed to slide round out of its original position the whole direction of the shot is affected. If the right foot comes up in line with the left, then there is little effect to the shot; however, in this case if you miss the ball you surely must know the consequences.

Batting demands that basic shots should be played properly, and any infringement of this technique will eventually lead to disaster. Now and then a risky shot is played and the result,

Figure 15 Lofted drive

like stolen fruit, is very sweet – but you will pay later.

A batsman who comes to mind immediately one thinks of technique is Sir Leonard Hutton whose ambition was to be a perfect stroke player, and who accomplished this wish to the full. His technique and approach to the game were even applauded and accepted by his Yorkshire colleagues! I doubt if Len ever knew how to play a bad shot. I certainly never saw him do so. In current cricket Glenn Turner, Worcestershire's New Zealander, is an outstanding example of correctness if without Sir Len's touch of genius. Turner started stodgily in English cricket and concentrated on technique. By 1970 his application flowered, and from the technique he was able to produce a wide range of scoring strokes all correctly played. He is one of our most consistent openers.

Returning to the straight drive over the bowler's head. This is another of those shots which causes so much controversy. One often hears from the older generation that the batsman should hit the ball over mid on and mid off. One particular enthusiast called for ' hard, high and often ' and then recalled the days of Frank Woolley and his illustrious contemporaries. If we had another Frank Woolley then I have no doubt that he would use these methods, and how everyone would enjoy it!

Unfortunately we do not have another Frank Woolley, and therefore we cannot expect everyone to play in this manner. With gifted players such as Gary Sobers, Graeme Pollock and Barry Richards we expect them to take this chance when the ball and time are favourable, but for the young cricketer who is struggling to get a place in the school side this lofted straight drive is courting trouble.

I cannot remember Sir Donald Bradman ever hitting a ball *over* mid off or mid on, and if you remember that he got 100 runs or more in an innings every three appearances at the crease, you will not attach too much importance to the ball hit in the air. If one is a skilful enough player to hit a good length ball into the air and to drop it where one wishes, then one is quite good enough to get many runs keeping the ball on the ground. If all half-volleys and long-hops were hit hard along the ground it would not be necessary to chance one's luck by hitting the ball in the air. If I had to coach a boy who hit the ball well and constantly in the air, and who was reasonably successful, I would not try to stop him from making these shots. But to teach the average boy to hit the ball in the air at all, is in my view bad coaching.

During a tour in Australia, in our first match versus Western Australia, Brian Close was batting. He had played an extremely fine knock and was in the eighties when he hit several shots for four over mid on and mid off. I was sitting near Len Hutton, watching the game, and was very surprised to hear his rather critical remarks about the ball in the air. Brian went on to get his century, and when eventually he was out he returned to well-deserved applause. However, it was not long before Len had a few words with him about those uppish shots in the eighties. At the time I thought Len a little hard on Brian, but now I am sure he was right.

Full Toss

To hit the full toss there are two methods. If the ball is fairly low – that is, just below knee height – it is better to play it with a straight bat and hit in the normal manner. Remember that the full toss may swing in the air and you are taking an unnecessary risk if you hit across the line. Anything above knee high and up to almost the head, and providing it is fairly in line with the leg side, can be played with a cross bat. The left leg should move well out and over to the line of the ball and the body well forward over a bent left knee. The bat is parallel to the

Figure 16 Hitting a full toss above knee-height

ground and at full-arm stretch, and when the ball is hit the wrists should be turned over to ensure that the ball goes down. When hitting to leg, try to hit in front of square leg as this will ensure solid contact with the ball. Do not try to hit too hard but keep balanced with head steady and eyes on the ball.

We have now to consider playing the attacking strokes off the back foot, and therefore we return to our foundation shot. This will enable us to get into the correct position to hit the ball.

Drive Off The Back Foot

This stroke is played to a ball pitching fairly short and straight. The bat is already picked up on the middle stump and the right foot should step back behind the line on which the ball pitched, with the head and body slightly forward over the ball, in exactly the same way as one would play the defensive shot. Instead of stopping the bat with the face slightly inclined to the ground, the bat is forced through the ball by the right hand and followed after, along the line the ball has now taken. The finish of this shot can either be with the face of the bat held high or with wrists turned over and arms fully extended, the momentum probably taking the bat over the left shoulder. Both finishes are made in the same manner as for the forward drive. One word of warning – make sure that arms are fully extended before turning back over left shoulder.

The shot can be played to a ball pitching from just outside the leg stump to one well clear of the off stump. In the case of a ball wide of the wickets the bat will not be quite so straight, but the angle will vary according to the width. This shot off the back foot played straight is very sound and is far safer than pulling the ball to the leg side across the line. If the ball pitches fairly wide outside the off stump, but is not wide enough to square cut, and we have our right foot correctly positioned on the off stump, we can if we wish play a forcing shot, or in the case of the ball moving back into the wicket we are perfectly placed to defend.

Figure 17 Drive off the back foot

Two fine players of this shot playing today are Clive Lloyd and Colin Cowdrey. I wonder if it is just a coincidence that they invariably finish so high in the batting averages? The sign of a very good player is that there is nothing ragged or hurried in the execution of his shots. Everything looks perfectly easy and he does not allow the right hand to overcome the guiding left.

Square Cuts

The square cut is played to a ball which pitches short and wide of the off stump, and generally from the fastish bowler. It should be hit when at the maximum height of its bounce. Although the bat is picked up in the normal manner, the batsman, when he appreciates that a bad ball has been bowled, will automatically pick his bat up a little higher. The shot is played with the bat horizontal, and it must come down on to the ball, otherwise the bat may get under the ball, resulting in a catch in the slips. The movement of the right foot depends entirely on the line of the ball. It must be placed to allow room for the arms and bat to come down on to the ball and pointing in the usual direction as in most back shots – towards gully or cover. The weight of the body is over the right leg with the head well to the fore. The ball is generally hit in the direction in which the right foot is pointing and this will depend on the speed and bounce of the ball. As in all shots, try to keep your head steady and do not hit too hard.

Many of the overseas players who are in county cricket today – Barry Richards, Glenn Turner, Intikhab, Younis Ahmed and Clive Lloyd, to name but a few – play this shot to a ball pitching very much straighter. They draw back almost on to the leg stump, giving themselves room, and then square cut almost off

Figure 18 Square cut off the back foot

the stumps. The reason for this is that pitches abroad, particularly in the West Indies, are true and fast, and the batsman knows that if the ball pitches short it will not deviate much and will bounce in an even manner. If one is used to playing this shot, a batsman might do it on a good pitch here but it will also cause him quite a lot of trouble. I feel sure these players find eventually that they have to adapt their shots to our conditions.

The Square Cut Off The Left Foot

This is not a shot often played, and I would hesitate to teach it to a young boy. My reason for not teaching it is that I like to emphasize, particularly to young cricketers, that one moves either forward to the ball pitching up, or back to the short ball. Going forward to a short ball does contradict and complicate things, at least for a beginner. For those who wish to know how this shot is played: the left foot is advanced to allow the very short and wide ball to be hit at the top of the bounce. The weight of the body is on the left foot and the right foot is grounded behind the popping crease. The execution of the shot is similar to the back foot shot with the bat coming down from a high back lift.

Late Cut

The late cut, if played properly, is a delightful shot to watch as the batsman uses the pace of the ball and ' nudges ' it on its way, rather than cracking it in the opposite direction. It is played off the back foot which is pointed behind gully or even second slip, the bat being brought down almost perpendicularly on top of the ball. The weight is mostly on the right leg and the head steady and leading the shot. I remember only one batsman who really *hit* the late cut. It was Keith Miller, and he used to chop the bat down very hard, often hitting the ground after the ball. Although he had the pleasure of a few sizzling fours, he got himself out in this way several times. I can remember him hitting his own wicket on one occasion when he was three runs short of his century. And I suppose that Kent's Brian Luckhurst and Clive Lloyd are now in the same class.

The Leg Glance

The leg glance, whether played on the front or back foot, is one of the more advanced shots, and unless it is played extremely well is very dangerous. Basically the shot is the same as the forward and back defensive shot, except that at the moment of impact the face of the bat is turned in the direction you wish the ball to go. One must take care to turn the ball only in the direction the ball is swinging. If the ball is in-swinging, it is a favourable ball to turn down the leg side, but it is risky to try to glance any ball going the other way. One can get runs

Figure 19 Leg glance off the back foot

by playing a leg glance off a good-length ball providing it is pitched near the leg stump, but this is not the shot for a beginner.

When playing the leg glance off the back foot, the right foot should go back into the wicket far enough to allow the ball to come down in line with the left leg, and it is then played as late as possible underneath the head. When played by a first-class player, this is a most useful shot and one that also causes some annoyance to the bowler, as it need not be a really bad delivery. It is a shot I would leave to the batsman to play when he has had a lot of experience and has confidence in himself to play it successfully.

Hitting The Leg Long-Hop

This shot, being much more natural, is one which can be taught even to the beginner. By this I do not mean only this shot, but after a session of rather boring defensive technique, to hit the ball hard in this manner is a useful safety valve. The young player will get many long-hops on the leg, and by knowing how to play this shot he will make runs which will allow him time to play the necessary straight bat shots.

The important thing is that the ball *must* pitch outside the leg stump; otherwise, if the ball pitches straight, no matter how short, it should be played with a straight bat. For the leg shot the right foot moves back into the wicket on about the middle stump, opening the body, and the left foot is put down in line with the ball and level with the right foot. The weight and poise of the body is forward, the bat is swung horizontally from a fairly high pick up and with arms at full stretch, and the ball is hit as the wrists turn over. Try to hit the ball in front of square leg and do not turn the head or body round to leg in making the shot. Keep looking at the spot where your bat contacted the ball. Many runs are missed on the leg side because the shot is played as the ball is going by the leg, instead of in front of the body. This shot is not dangerous as long as it is played to the

D

Figure 20 Hitting the leg long-hop

ball pitching outside the leg stump, and I repeat *not* to a straight ball.

The Hook Shot

Although the hook shot is played in exactly the same way as the hit to leg, the difference is in the position of the ball. The hook shot can be very dangerous particularly from a fast bowler, and only the very good player should attempt this shot. It is played to a straight ball, even to one pitching on the off stump although it must be very short. The right foot should be moved back and across the wicket far enough to take the head just outside the line of the ball. The ball is hit from a high back lift and with a horizontal bat, turning the wrists over at impact to keep the ball down.

I have seen a number of accidents as the result of the hook shot and I would advise the young player not to be too rash,

Figure 21 The finish of the hook stroke

and to take care when attempting the hook. I am not suggesting you should not hook, but practise with a comparatively slow bowler at first and gradually increase the pace. Start playing the shot by hooking on the leg side and then move by degrees across the stumps, so that you build up your confidence. Do not try to hook any ball which pitches outside the off stump or one that is above head high.

The Sweep Shot

The sweep to leg is probably played today more than it has ever been. If the ball is hit correctly, there is little chance of it going into the air, but so often, particularly by boys, it is not, and the ball often goes up towards square leg.

The ball should be hit on the half-volley with a horizontal bat and the wrists turned over at impact. It is played in a similar manner as the shot to the full toss on the leg, with the left leg well forward, and reaching with the arm out to the pitch. So often a boy sees that a ball is on the leg side and, without thought as to its length, he just hoicks at it round the corner. The chances are that he misses it completely, and perhaps this is just as well, as more than likely it would go into the air.

Concentration And Application

Under this heading lies much that is really necessary in all departments of the game. Batting most certainly needs its share of both: to concentrate on the ball and the length it pitches, and to apply the technique that has been taught. What a tremendous difference these two qualities have made in deciding the fate and careers of many young players. Pure ability has at times not been enough when the other two qualities were lacking, and of course the reverse has also happened. This does not only concern batting, as bowling also needs a measure of these two qualities.

Running Between The Wickets

Running between the wickets in school cricket can be very hazardous and great care must be taken in trying to teach boys how to take every short single. I am sure that the standard can be improved, but only by continual practice. Just to tell boys to take short singles is asking for trouble. Every player must be fully aware that the side is looking for the short single, and they must be ready, backing up, and if called must go at once. Correct calling is essential. It is the striker's call if the ball goes square, or in front, of square, on either side of the wicket. It is his partner's call if the ball goes behind the wicket. For subsequent runs it is the call of the batsman who is running towards the wicket nearer to the fielder with, or who is chasing, the ball.

The call is ' Yes ', ' No ', or ' Wait '. *Wait* means you might take one, and you should end the call by either *Yes* or *No*. Always run the first run quickly; you can then see if a second or third is possible and call again if necessary.

The non-striker should stand outside the crease with his bat placed on the ground inside the popping crease. He should stand on the opposite side of the stumps from the bowler. After the ball has been delivered he may move a yard or two down the pitch in readiness for a run, or to return to his crease. It is better for the non-striker to hold his bat in his left hand if the bowler is bowling over the wicket (right hand) but it can be changed to the right hand if the ball is played to the off side, or kept in the left hand if the ball is played to the on side. This will help the batsman to see where the ball has gone and will enable him to decide more quickly if another run is possible. When you reach the popping crease, do not bang the bat down but run it in on the ground over the line, or, if you are taking another run, place it quite deliberately beyond the popping crease; this will give the umpire a better chance of making a correct decision in the case of a run out appeal. A warning to the striker: even when you have hit the ball smack with the middle of your bat and it has gone like a bomb into the covers, make sure that it has gone past the fielder before you go for a run. If in doubt, call ' Wait ' and then confirm. Watch out for misfields; they may be a trap for the unwary batsman.

It must be remembered by the batsmen that if they have taken several sharp singles and appear to be eager to get the extra run, the fielding side will be on their toes, and although I am very much in favour of getting every possible run, a run is never worth a wicket.

' Walking '

Although I hardly think it is necessary to remind anyone of the fact, it is considered part of the spirit of the game that if you *know* you have hit the ball and you *know* you have been caught, you should walk back to the pavilion. There is absolutely no doubt in my mind about this. But if you are *not* sure either about the catch or whether you have hit the ball, then I think you are entitled to ask for the umpire's decision.

A Batting Resumé

I feel sure that having read so far you will have come to the opinion that I am what one would call in today's jargon ' a cricket square '. I believe that the bat should be picked up straight and brought down straight; that whenever possible a straight bat should be used; that one should try to keep the ball on the ground, and that to do this the body must be sideways on to the line of the ball, and the face of the bat shown to the ball as long as possible. Hit the half-volley and long-hop hard, and play a sound defensive shot to the good-length ball. Play each ball according to its merit and be careful of anticipating the bowler's intention. Pay attention to detail, such as keeping the right toe down on the forward shot. If you are playing a defensive shot, then make sure you stop the bat going through. If you decide to hit, then go right through the ball at full arms' stretch. Do not cut off the off stump or sweep off the middle; there are more sound ways of dealing with these balls. Watch the ball. Run the first run quickly.

4
Bowling

Bowling is very enjoyable and I am sure that unless you do enjoy it you may never reach any standard. You must look forward to your next net and be disappointed if you are taken off or not put on to bowl. When I was at the Faulkner Cricket School and I happened to get to work early, the Major would reward me with an hour's bowling. This of course gave me great delight which I suppose must have been obvious because on one particular day I remember him saying, ' Now, Wright, a net at 2.30 p.m. and don't get so excited.' I have often thought of this, particularly after toiling all day in the sun, and wished that I could regain some of the keenness which I felt in those days.

Bowlers win matches; I think most people will agree with this. ' Bowlers are born and not made '; I am not sure that this is quite so unanimous, although I cannot remember any success-ful bowler who had a poor action. There is a technique for bowling and the best results are obtained when the fundamentals are complied with. There are exceptions to every rule such as the bowler who bowls off the wrong (right) foot, such as Procter of Gloucestershire. However, he bowls well not because of this action, but in spite of it.

For the moment let us consider bowling a ball straight, without swing or spin. To do this we must first grip the ball in the basic grip – the seam held upright and pointing at the batsman, the index finger placed on the left side of the seam, the second finger just on the other side of the seam and the thumb under-neath. The ball is held in the fingers and not in the palm of the hand. We have now got our grip correct and have decided to

Figure 22 The grip

bowl a ball of medium pace, and therefore we do not need a long run-up. Perhaps eight paces will be long enough and we must make sure of running straight to the wicket. On the last stride of the run-up, we jump off the left foot and turn the body to face the side of the stumps. In doing this our left arm is pushed up well above the head, and we look towards the batsman over the left side of the arm. The body is tilted slightly backwards so that all the weight will now be on the right foot which is now parallel to the bowling crease.

As we jump off the left foot the ball in the right hand is held close to the face, and as the action unfolds the right hand is brought down to the right leg and is then pushed back in a wide arc in readiness to deliver the ball. The actual delivery occurs as the left leg hits the ground. All the weight is now on the left leg which is braced to take the force of the right arm, which should be held as high as possible. After releasing the ball the arm should reach out towards the batsman and then carry on passing the left hip. Every effort should be made to keep the head up and eyes on the batsman, long after delivering the ball.

Grip

The grip is changed according to the ball you wish to bowl.

Run-Up

The object of the run-up is to bring the bowler to the bowling crease with the necessary momentum to deliver the ball at the pace he requires. Start your run slowly and gradually increase your pace until you jump into your action. It is advisable to run straight to the wicket as this helps the transfer of weight during the action.

Basic Action

Position 1

The last stride of the run-up before the delivery stride is a jump off the left foot. The right foot and body start to turn sideways, the left arm is stretching upwards and the right hand with the ball is close to the face.

Figure 23 Bowling – Position 1

Position 2

The right foot has landed parallel to the crease, and the body has turned so that the left shoulder points to the batsman. The left arm pushes upwards, the weight is now on the right foot, and the body leaning back. The head is steady and upright, looking down the wicket over the left arm. The left leg is raised slightly off the ground.

These two positions are the 'winding up' of the action and the following two positions 'the release'.

Before Position 3 comes the delivery stride. This is made with the left foot and should be as straight as possible down the wicket, keeping your foot in a natural position and pointing the toes to fine leg.

Figure 24 Bowling – Position 2   Figure 25 Bowling – Position 3

Position 3

As the left leg hits the ground the leg is braced to take all the weight and also the force of the right arm delivering the ball. The head is kept up and the right arm goes out towards the batsman after delivering the ball and then on to the left hip of the bowler.

Position 4

The pivot has now completed, we are still on the left leg, the right hand has gone by the bowler's left hip, the head is still up and looking at the batsman. Finally we will follow through according to the speed we have bowled.

So many boys have been told to follow through as if this is all that mattered. In fact it matters very little, as it should be the

Figure 26 Bowling – Position 4

result of a sound bowling action. A sound bowling action will give you a straight follow through, but a 'follow through' will never give you a sound action. I have met many boys who have followed through for some considerable distance and have almost caught up with the ball they have bowled. There is a real danger in over-emphasizing the follow through: the bowler may not pay enough attention to stopping on a braced left leg, and because of this he will lose much of his speed and 'nip' off the pitch. This is a fault which I am continually having to try to correct.

The glut of in-swing bowlers in first-class cricket is influencing the style adopted by many of today's schoolboys. Every other boy who bowls is either in-swinging or bowling from wide of the crease and aiming down the leg side. After questioning these boys as to why they were trying to bowl in-swingers, most of them seemed ignorant of what they were doing. This method of bowling will very quickly ruin a boy's action as it causes him to fall away to the left on the delivery stride.

The foundation of batting is a correct forward and back defensive shot, and the foundation of bowling is the *action*. From jumping off the left foot to the follow through of the right hand past the left leg is vital. If this does not come easily or naturally, every effort should be made to improve it, and even if you already have a good action you should constantly watch to see that it does not change. Whether you wish to bowl fast, medium or slow will depend mostly on your 'action'. It is a wrong assumption to say that because a bowler is tall and strong he will necessarily bowl fast. Many of the best fast bowlers have not been very tall, but of average height, and have certainly not been muscle men. The fast bowler depends so much on his action as speed is his main weapon. He will also endeavour to make the ball swing and cut the ball off the seam. Ray Lindwall – the great Australian fast bowler – was very versatile, as he could, at times, swing the ball away from the batsman, and bowl extremely quickly. Today there is something of a dearth of bowlers of Lindwall's ability but Procter of

Gloucestershire, John Snow and, of course, Sobers have almost the same gift.

During a Test match in Australia, I had to go in to ' stop a hat-trick ' when Ray Lindwall was bowling. I knew that he would not bowl me a ' bumper ', as he rarely did this against the latter batsmen. It was, in fact, the finest away swinger that I have ever played at – and missed! It started swinging from just outside the leg stump, pitched on and whipped by my off stump. I played back, which probably saved me, as if I had gone forward I might have been good enough to get an edge!

There is something of interest for the away swing bowler in this story. Lindwall's action was slightly lower than vertical and I said, the ball started swinging from just outside the leg stump, and even then it swung too much and missed the off stump. With a very high action, I doubt if the ball would swing too much, particularly if aimed just on the leg stump. This is *not* a criticism of Lindwall's bowling, as he was a very fine bowler.

Gary Sobers, Graham McKenzie, Allan Ward and John Snow can all use the ball at speed and have fine actions. Of past heroes Trueman, Statham, Larwood and Tyson all had this ability. All such bowlers can get wickets by speed alone, although, of course, to make the ball ' do ' something as well heightens their performance and ability.

Extra speed comes from using the left arm more in pushing the body back on to the right foot, and lifting the left foot higher; in whacking the left foot down and releasing the ball and bracing the left leg, letting the right hand thud against the back on the follow through. There is no guile in this, just brute force, coupled with timing and rhythm. Action really matters to the fast bowler.

The medium-pace bowler must find another weapon to compensate for not being able, by pure pace, to get wickets. Firstly he must have an action that will enable him to bowl accurately for long spells. He must also be able to swing the ball, at least one way, and cut the ball back off the seam. This is the minimum expected of the seam bowler. The compensating weapon is that he must be far more accurate than the fast bowler, and when a pitch is favourable to his type of bowling he must make full use of it. No other bowler has played this role more successfully than Alec Bedser whose successors today could well be Eddie Barlow of South Africa or Peter Lever of Lancashire off his shortened run.

Next we have the slow bowler. Although the action does matter, the slow bowler does not rely on it quite so much as the fast and medium-pace bowlers. In most cases, the slow bowler needs to ' spin ' the ball, and have a sufficiently good action to keep the ball up to the batsman.

When one bowls either off-spin or leg-spin on an average type of pitch, the emphasis is not to hit the pitch with the ball as one would when bowling fast, but to throw the ball *up* and let the ball bounce. This calls for a slight difference in the mechanics of the action. The difference is that although the right hand must, after delivery, continue to follow through to the left side, the ball is released a little earlier in a slightly upward direction.

I mentioned the ' average ' pitch, as on a wet pitch it is sometimes advisable to bring the ball down and make use of conditions, even when bowling leg-spinners. In this case the action is used a little more like the seam bowler, releasing the ball a little later to bring it down and make it hit the ground.

To sum up the requirements for a fast bowler, one should be fairly strong, slightly above medium height, possess a fairly good action and have a fairly fiery temperament. The ' action ' is of utmost importance to the fast bowler, although one should be able to swing the ball and make it move off the seam. The medium-pace bowler relies not only on a steady action but on length and direction, coupled with swing and cut. Whereas the fast bowler can get away with the occasional bad ball, the medium-pacer must keep it ' there ', and to get wickets he must make the ball really ' do ' something. He cannot afford to show too much temperament, as he has not the pace to worry a batsman.

The slow bowler must be patient, philosophical and hard-working. Although the action does matter, as of course it matters to all bowlers, it is not quite so important. What really matters is that one can 'spin' the ball, and keep it on a length. I emphasize in the first place 'spin', and spin it as much as you possibly can, because you will *not* spin it too much. It is quite useless bowling with straight fingers and concentrating on length and then saying, 'Now I will spin it.' There is a different trajectory when you spin the ball, which gives a different length and in most cases it should pitch slightly closer to the batsman.

Many boys do not have any of the necessary attributes; they can neither spin, swing nor cut the ball, and often their actions are sadly lacking in rhythm and technique. To coach these boys one must seek out any natural ability they may have and then build upon this.

Length and Direction

A good-length ball is one which bounces in such a position on the pitch that it presents the batsman with the problem of whether to go forward to play it as it pitches, or to go back. This may seem quite a straightforward explanation but, in fact, to define it satisfactorily it is not easy. Length depends on so many things: the speed of the bowler, the pace of the pitch, how much the ball is turning and, to some extent, the height of the batsman. The good-length ball lies between a full-pitch and a long-hop. The fast bowler on a hard pitch will have a margin of error of about six feet. This means that the bowler can pitch the ball from about six feet from the batsman up to twelve feet away and the batsman will be forced to defend either forward or back. In the case of a slow bowler spinning the ball a lot on a slow pitch, the margin of error is much less, possibly as little as two feet; that is, four feet to six feet from the batsman. The more the ball turns, the farther up it must be pitched to be of good length.

A full-pitch is one which the batsman can hit from the crease before it pitches. A half-volley is one which he can hit just after

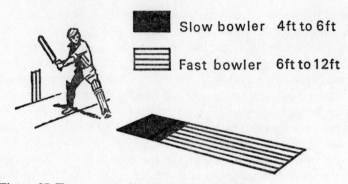

Slow bowler　4ft to 6ft

Fast bowler　6ft to 12ft

Figure 27 Target areas for good-length bowling

it has bounced. A good-length ball is one which bounces a little shorter than a half-volley, and if the batsman tries to hit it from the crease it will quite likely go into the air. A long-hop is a short ball easily seen off the pitch; it should always be punished. The tall batsman can, of course, reach farther down the pitch and this will reduce the margin of error, at least to the upper limit. However, nature seems to compensate the short batsman for his lack of reach: he is often quicker on his feet and has more room and time to hook and cut the ball. The diminutive Harry Pilling of Lancashire is a fine contemporary example. Length, from a bowler's point of view, is to try to make the batsman play forward without achieving a scoring shot. For a batsman to make a safe scoring shot forward, the ball would have to be a half-volley. A ball bowled short gives the batsman too much time to see and get into a position to score. There are two goods reasons for keeping the batsman playing forward; one is that the ball can move off the pitch between the bounce of the ball and meeting the bat; the other that a ball kept as long as possible in the air has time to alter its direction. Length for the batsman means he must be ready to move his front foot as near as possible to the pitch in going forward or to step back well behind the ball.

When I started bowling leg-breaks I bowled at quite a slow

pace, but found great difficulty in keeping a length. To increase my margin of error I quickened my pace until I came to the limit of my speed. There is more to bowling leg-breaks than mere pace; trajectory is one thing which governs speed – however, more about this later.

One rather amusing true story about length. I was bowling in a county match and was just about to deliver the ball when the batsman stepped aside and tried to remove a worm from the pitch. As he took some time in doing this, a voice from the slips was heard to say, 'Leave it on a length – it will be quite safe there!'

Direction

Although length is vital it must be coupled with direction. To bowl a length with direction is the only way to make the most of the field set. Some batsmen are very strong on the off and others on the leg and a bowler must be able to attack where necessary. Direction *is* important.

I would not consider bowling to either Gary Sobers or Graeme Pollock on the off side, even with an off-side field. The lesser of the two evils would be to bowl at the leg stump to both of these players. Sometimes I tried to bowl to Denis Compton without an extra-cover and concentrate on the middle and leg stump, as although he would play his sweep shot to anything near the leg, there was a chance it might go into the air. There was little chance of his making a poor shot on the off side.

Swing and Swerve

The ball can be made to swing in the air, either away from the batsman or in to him. On some days, when there is a lot of humidity, the ball will swing appreciably more than on a dry sunny day. The amount of wind and the direction it is blowing will also have a certain effect on how much the ball will move. Why the ball does swing is a question that I do not intend trying to answer here. I know how to make a ball swerve and on most

E

days I could swing it either in or out, but to explain why is something which has baffled many mathematicians, if not the theorists. The ball will swing far more when it is either new or has not completely lost the shine, and the seam is still fairly prominent. While it is not unlawful for the bowler to shine the ball, raising the seam is frowned upon and should be stopped.

Grip – Away Swing The ball is held between the first two fingers and the thumb, with the seam upright, the index finger on the left side of the seam and the second finger just placed on the other side with the thumb under the ball and on the seam. The seam should point to the batsman, and the shiny side of the ball now faces the on side.

Action The action already described should be kept to, with particular emphasis on the right hand going past the left leg. Try to keep the fingers behind the ball for as long as possible. Do *not* alter your delivery stride, but keep it straight down the pitch. Any alteration by placing the left foot to either side can easily cause a lot of trouble with the action. One first class bowler, who must remain anonymous, placed his left foot too far to the on side in the delivery stride; it completely ruined his action, and eventually he had to give the game up.

I would suggest that the bowler experiments with pointing the seam slightly in the direction of first slip. This may help move the ball a little more. The ball will swing by lowering the height of the arm, but it will also start to swing much earlier and of course will therefore be seen by the batsman more easily. The best ball is bowled by a high-arm action, as this will swing much later. However much you experiment (and this is a good thing) do not allow your basic action to deteriorate.

The more the ball swings, the farther up it will be necessary to pitch it and one should try to make the batsman play forward. There is so much more chance that the batsman will not really get to the pitch when playing forward, but if the ball is short he will have more time to see and play it. If the ball is swinging a lot, there are several methods of controlling it –

Figure 28 Grip for the away

Figure 29 Grip for the in-swerve

one is to keep the arm high, another is to use the crease. Bowling wide of the crease and 'directing' the ball to the leg will counteract any excessive swerve. What is far more likely is that one cannot swing the ball enough, and in this case one should deliver as close as possible to the stumps, and aim at the off stump, although ideally one should bowl a good length pitching on the middle. Remember to go well by your left side with the right hand.

In-swerve Whether it is easier to bowl the in-swerve than the away swinger is perhaps a matter of opinion but I am quite certain that far more harm can be done to an action by trying to bowl in-swerves than by any other method of bowling.

The ball can be held in almost the same way as for the out-swerve, except that the shiny side should face the opposite direction (off side) with the seam pointing very slightly in the direction of fine leg. The bowler can alter the angle of the seam to suit his own ' action' but I am not convinced that this is so very important.

The delivery stride should be almost straight; perhaps the

left foot can be placed very slightly towards the off side, to allow the body and arm to come through straight. I must repeat that to allow the left foot to stray too far either side of the straight line will cause a lot of trouble. The right hand should swing well through past the *right* leg, and the follow through should be straight. Do not allow the body to fall away to the off side.

Try to do with your right arm, when bowling, what you wish the ball to do in the air. When bowling the in-swerve, make sure you are fairly close to the return crease, as this will help with direction. If you bowl close to the wicket and have to aim the ball outside the off stump, you may find difficulty in making the ball swing. Do not complicate things when you are learning. Try to use every aid to keep a length and swing the ball. Once you have mastered the knack of swinging the ball, you can experiment with direction.

To bowl an in-swerve, the right hand must go slightly past the *vertical* position and towards the leg in an arc which will take the hand past the right leg. For the away-swerve the right hand must go slightly past the vertical and towards the off side in an arc which will take the hand past the left leg. I am quite certain it is the initial pushing of the ball in the direction you wish it to swing that is the most important part of the delivery. If one bowls with a low arm for the away swinger, the ball is obviously pushed more than if bowled with a high arm.

Off-Spin

The off-spin bowler aims to pitch the ball on the off side and bring it back into the wicket. Depending on how much the pitch is responding to spin, will it be necessary to alter the direction. The off-spin bowler must not be confused with the off-cutter, as it is not possible to bowl the spinner quickly whereas the cutter can be bowled quite fast. There is one point I would like to make about all types of spin or cut bowling.

Glenn Turner, the New Zealand opening batsman now playing for Worcestershire. After a somewhat uncertain start to his county cricket career his patiently acquired technique allied to natural skill flowered in 1970 when Turner blossomed into an attractive free-scoring batsman, setting a county record of ten centuries in the season

The English Schools Cricket Association provides a vital link between up and coming youngsters and the county game. One of the highlights of the Association's programme is an annual match, pictured here, against MCC Young Professionals at Lord's

Grace, rhythm and controlled fury by John Snow, the England fast bowler who put the cream of Australia's batting to rout in the fourth Test at Sydney during the 1970-71 MCC tour. Note the high arm action, firm left leg and the use of the crease at the moment before delivery

Fine action and follow-through by young Bob Willis of Surrey of whom England expects great things in the seasons to come

Graeme Pollock, the great South African left-hand batsman, forces the ball away on the offside, playing off the back foot. Allan Knott is the 'keeper in this 1970 unofficial Test against The Rest of the World which replaced the cancelled tour of England by South Africa

Yorkshire's Don Wilson and probably the best slow left-arm bowler playing in English cricket today. The follow-through position is a model for all budding bowlers of this type. Wilson is also a brilliant fieldsman and a hard hitting batsman

Perfect combined power and timing exemplified by Barry Richards of South Africa and Hampshire, the best batsman in the world today. After the Rest of the World *v* England series in 1970, Richards spent the winter playing for South Australia in Sheffield Shield and other matches where he devastated all bowlers sent against him, including the MCC tourists

The greatest all-rounder . . . Garfield St Aubyn Sobers demonstrates one of his many cricketing facets, bowling fast left arm over the wicket with the new ball. Also known as a fine purveyor of slow left-arm orthodox and 'chinaman' spin, brilliant close to the wicket fielder and, of course, one of the finest batsmen in the world, Sobers who captains West Indies and Nottinghamshire, is the complete cricketing genius – but his technique is perfect, too

Shorn of his introspective tendencies, Colin Cowdrey of Kent and England must surely have added much more to his already near-record list of successes. Here he forces the ball away on the off-side, an object lesson in timing and positioning for any cricketer

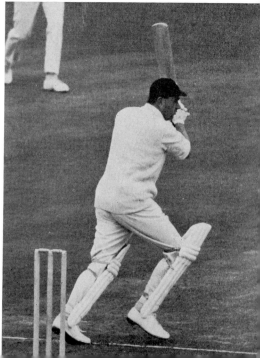

The bowler may spin and cut the ball for all he is worth yet the ball may not move. It all depends on the state of the pitch, that is, whether there is much movement or not. To try to regulate the amount of spin may sound a very professional way of bowling, but I have never met anyone who regularly spun the ball too much – most people wished they could spin it more.

Off-spin bowling is a natural way of bowling; if you swing your arm over, you will find that the palm of the hand usually faces the body as it comes down. This is the direction of the off-spinner's hand as he spins the ball and as the arm follows through to his left side. Although the action does matter, it is not absolutely vital that it should be a classic movement, providing the bowler can spin the ball and pitch it more or less where he wants to.

I am sure that it does help to have a ' high arm ' when bowling off-spinners as one can get a nice oval trajectory which entices a batsman forward. If one's arm is low, one gets a flatter trajectory, the length of which is not quite so difficult for the batsman to judge. On a very good pitch, where the ball will only turn a little (if at all), the bowler needs to use the air and this can be done much better, and more easily, if the arm is high. There is of course, an exception to every rule. If one studies the actions and the right-arm position of the top off-spin bowlers of the past such as Jim Laker, Tom Goddard, Ramadhin and Jack Iverson, or Pat Pocock, Fred Titmus and Lance Gibbs in contemporary cricket, one will notice that their right arm is very high and that they all bowl at very much the same pace. The speed governs the trajectory: one must not bowl too quickly or one will lose flight, or so slowly as to allow the batsman successfully to make ground to you. I remember a Kent off-spin bowler who really could spin the ball but unfortunately could not raise his arm very high. This made him bowl with a very flat trajectory, and although he was successful on a damp wicket, where the ball turned a lot, he was not so satisfactory when the pitch was hard and true. The off-spin is a downward motion, and a low arm does restrict the height one can bowl.

Grip I have often heard it said that 'old So-and-So' has enormous fingers and a hand like a shovel, and that is why he can spin the ball so much. I really am not sure that it is so important to have such large hands. If you have been bowling with the normal full-size ball (5½ oz) and then find yourself bowling with a boy's ball (4¾ oz) you will find that the fingers do not fit into place as they usually do on the full-size ball. I have always found that the small ball is, in fact, too small to grip properly. I remember Tom Goddard bowling; he had very large hands, and I must admit he spun the ball a great deal, but I also remember Tich Freeman who had the smallest fingers I have seen on a man.

I am inclined to think that what matters is not so much the size of the fingers as the elasticity and feeling in them. Some people have this more than others. This of course must be coupled with wrist, arm and action all working as one. So, if you have fairly strong, average-size fingers, do not despair, as you may be able to spin the ball as well as anyone.

The off-break is spun in a clockwise direction from left to right, the ball being held between the first two fingers, the two others being curled slightly over the ball, with the thumb on the opposite side. The main finger, the index finger, is dug into one side of the seam, and the second finger far enough away

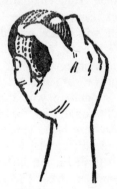

Figure 30 Grip for the off-break

to exert some purchase on the first finger. If the two fingers are too close together there will be very little leverage, and if too far apart they will interfere with the easy flow of the ball from the fingers. Each person should find the correct distance between first and second fingers according to the size of his hand. Do *not* force the ball between the fingers, or use a grip which does not feel comfortable. The ball can be held with the fingers round the seam, or across, providing the top joint of the first finger can get some pull on the ball.

The right arm should be taken right back, making a full sweep. As the arm comes over, the right wrist is cocked; the palm will now be facing upwards and the thumb pointing to the off. On delivery, the hand flips forward and through 180 degrees, the thumb now pointing to the *on* side with the palm uppermost. The 'action' should finish in exactly the same way as the basic action, although, if care is taken not to go too far, the left foot may be placed *slightly* towards the leg side, to enable a little more drag to be put on the body; this is transmitted to the arm and, eventually, through the first finger, to the ball.

Let me repeat once again that any large alteration in the placing of the feet in the delivery stride will cause real trouble. It would probably be much safer if the delivery stride were always straight. I am sure that the little good that any alteration does is outweighed by the damage it can cause. To bowl the off-spinner well, or in fact, to bowl any type of bowling, one must have a certain rhythm. From the run up to the action and follow through, it must all move easily, everything synchronizing perfectly, yet not without energy and whip.

Bowling Off-Spinners

'What is the wicket like?' The answer to this question may mean quite a lot to you, an off-spin bowler. Let us imagine it to be hard, fast and true. The ball will hardly deviate, let alone turn, but at least it does do it quickly. The opponents are an average team, quite able to get a fair score on this type of pitch.

Firstly, as we cannot hope to get much help from the pitch, we must make use of the air. This does not mean we have got to slow right down, and throw up half-volleys, but to change the pace a little more often.

The line of attack should be on or just outside the off stump, with an off side field set, which should make it very difficult to score on the off side. The actual field setting must be very fluid, according to the control of the bowler and the ability of the batsman. If the bowler's arm is kept as high as possible he will get a nice oval trajectory, which is what we want for this type of pitch. Constantly change the pace, which will mean releasing one a little early to get height, and pushing another through – or holding on. Another sound scheme is to vary direction (but never getting too close to the leg side). Remember to throw one a little higher and a little wider – make sure cover is not too close. I am not in favour of bowling a ball from well behind the crease, as I have never seen it done successfully; it has usually gone for four. However, I do believe in changing to go round the wicket, even on a good pitch. You may have to make a slight alteration in the field setting, but the bowler should try to keep towards the off side.

I once saw a remarkable piece of bowling done by Tom Goddard in South Africa. It was during a Test Match at Johannesburg. South Africa were batting on a beautiful wicket, and the ball would hardly grip at all. The runs were coming quite steadily. Dudley Nourse, who was a fine player, had scored 73 not out. Tom had been bowling over the wicket, with the normal off-side field, trying, if possible, to keep the runs down. He was not too happy about this as he believed in attacking, so he switched to bowling round the wicket. The result was quite astounding: in his first over round the wicket he did the hat-trick, getting Nourse caught and bowled by the first ball, a stumping with the second, and clean bowled with the third. I cannot quite decide on why he got the c & b but the stumping was obviously a ball that 'went with his arm', and a similar thing happened to the third, both batsmen playing for the turn. If the batsmen get used to the angle at which you are bowling, try an over or two from the opposite side of the wicket.

So much for the hard and true pitch. Now for the helpful, turning wicket. Whatever you do, you must keep the ball up and make the batsman play forward. To bowl on this type of wicket is not as easy as it sounds. The more a ball turns, the farther up it must be pitched and therefore the smaller the area of error. Now that the lbw law has been altered yet again it is advisable to bowl round the wicket whenever the ball really turns, as this will allow you to pitch on and straighten or even bring the ball back to get a decision.

Field placing for any bowling must depend on where the bowler pitches the ball, the state of the pitch and the ability of the batsman. Whenever you are bowling on a bad wicket, concentrate *only* on keeping a length and the pitch will do the rest for you. The very fact that you are spinning the ball will give you enough variation. Some of the best off-spin bowlers have produced a ball which ' goes the other way '; in fact they have bowled a leg break or leg cutter. The great difficulty is in disguising it, as if it is seen it has lost most of its worth. Even a ball which does not turn, yet is bowled with a similar wrist movement as the off-spin, can prove useful. Ramadhin, who played for the West Indies, apart from bowling a very well flighted off break, also bowled a cut leg break which turned on most pitches, and was very difficult to spot, and Jack Iverson of Australia also produced a similar ball. Iverson, who bowled with a rather unorthodox grip, was nevertheless an extremely fine bowler who spun the off-break considerably. Australia's Johnnie Gleeson has the same technique as indeed, in his own fashion, has Lance Gibbs, of Warwickshire.

A rather interesting story about Tom Goddard of Gloucester is that he started his bowling career as a fast bowler. He played for MCC and then Gloucester where, not being successful, he changed his method of bowling to off-spin and had tremendous success. This is rather an interesting point for those who are concerned with coaching. One must find out as quickly as possible the hidden talents that the pupil may have. It is sometimes a sound plan to ask the bowler to try to bowl all types of ball and also to find out whether or not he is a useful bat. Brian Luckhurst, the Kent and England opening bat, came on the Kent staff as a left-arm bowler, and credit is due to Claude Lewis (the Kent coach at that time) for giving him the necessary technique, and to Luckhurst for applying himself so readily and successfully. One other very fine cricketer, Derek Shackleton, started as a batsman for Hampshire and finished as one of the best medium-pace bowlers in the country. Another point regarding Luckhurst: he has a very nice easy action, and could bowl a respectable length but unfortunately he could not really spin it.

Leg Breaks, Top Spinners and Googlies

Perhaps I am rather prejudiced in favour of this type of bowling, but to me there is nothing to compare with this method of attack. Before electing to struggle with the leg break it is essential that you should be able to ' spin the ball ' quite a lot and naturally. Having established this essential fact, one must also be prepared to accept a certain amount of punishment without being unduly worried; in fact, it might act as a stimulant.

Although a perfect action is not essential, it is still a very useful adjunct, and it will probably improve your bowling if you have a high action. However, if you can *spin* the ball and yet have an action not considered completely orthodox, do not worry for, as I have said before, it is not so vitally necessary. The leg break is the stock ball while the top spinner and googly are surprise weapons.

For well over 30 years I have seen, and in many cases played against, leg-break bowlers in England and from overseas, and in all that time I have seen only one bowler who could really bowl a first-class top spinner. This was A. P. Freeman of Kent, who bowled it a little quicker than his leg break; it seemed to gather pace off the pitch. I think that in many cases the batsman had played back when he should have gone forward owing to the lower trajectory, and in this case the ball does appear to nip through quickly. Tich Freeman must have got many hundreds of wickets with this ball.

I always found the top spinner very difficult to bowl – in fact I used it very rarely. The googly (an off-break with a leg-break action) is much more easy to bowl than the top spinner and a more satisfying delivery as it will either turn or bounce and sometimes both. The purpose of the googly is as a surprise ball, although I cannot see why it should not be used as a stock ball if you can control it sufficiently. I do not think it is more difficult to bowl than the leg break, but if you are bowling it as a surprise ball every effort must be made to conceal the fact. This is the difficult part of the googly. Do *not* alter your action in any way, as this will soon be noticed by the batsman.

For the young bowler interested in leg breaks I would suggest that he concentrates on his basic bowling action, particularly the high arm and follow through past the left leg, spinning the ball and bowling a length (with direction). Do not worry about changing pace and using the crease yet; this can come later on. Experiment in the nets with the top spinner and googly, but before doing so you must thoroughly understand what you are doing with your wrist and arm. I have had many people come to me and say they used to bowl quite a good leg break but can now bowl only the googly. This is often caused by trying to spin the ball *too* much, and not knowing exactly what they are doing.

In common with the off-spin bowler, when the pitch is hard and true the ball must be thrown up, and when it is wet and sticky one should push the ball through. It may interest you to know that when bowling on a hard and fast pitch often the leg break would turn very little and yet the googly would sometimes turn and bounce. The leg break is spun with the fingers over the ball, and in most cases the ball is going in the direction of the spin. With the googly, the ball is bowled out of the back of the hand and upwards, and is spun in the opposite direction from that which the arm is taking. The result is, as I have said, that the googly bounces much more than the leg break. The reaction of the ball to a wet and sticky pitch is almost the opposite. The leg break, bowled with the fingers over the ball and in a somewhat downward motion, penetrates the surface of the wicket and turns quickly. The googly thrown out of the back of the hand, and generally in an upward direction, does not hit the pitch quite so hard and will plop rather than turn or bounce.

Grip for the Leg Break The orthodox grip for the leg break is as follows: the ball is held in the first three fingers, which are spaced comfortably apart. The top joint of the third finger, which is under the ball, takes most of the pressure. The thumb,

Figure 31 Grip for the leg break

which has very little part in spinning the ball, rests naturally on the seam. The ball should be held quite firmly. The wrist is bent to almost ninety degrees and the back of the hand is uppermost. On delivery, the ball is spun off the third finger by the synchronization of the action plus the flicking and twisting of the wrist in an anti-clockwise direction. For the greatest spin, the right arm should be fully extended, with a large arc of swing, finishing in a full follow through past the left leg. The back of the right hand must be uppermost throughout the swing, as this will ensure that you will bowl a leg break.

If you are one of those who cannot bowl a leg break, just a googly, make sure the next time you bowl that the back of your right hand is kept facing the sky, and if you can spin the ball at all, you will bowl a leg break.

To bowl a top spinner, you have got to turn the arm until the hand, if held upright, is sideways on to the batsman. If the ball is held in the same way, with the wrist bent to ninety degrees, the seam of the ball will not be pointing straight down the pitch to the batsman. On delivery the wrist is flicked straight and the right arm pushed through towards the batsman, and the follow through should take the right hand to the left knee.

Googly The googly is an off break with a leg-break action. The ball is held in exactly the same manner as for the leg break, with the wrist turned down to ninety degrees. The arm is turned in an anti-clockwise direction with the back of the hand now pointing towards the batsman. As the wrist is flicked straight, the ball will come out of the back of the hand over the third finger. There is no need to alter your action the slightest bit. Do not drop the left shoulder or point the left foot. If you have to make any alteration at all in the way you bowl the googly, you can be quite certain that someone will notice it, and in only a short time it will be well known.

To make quite sure that you know how to bowl a leg break, top spinner or googly, I will try to simplify it for you. Hold the ball in the correct grip and raise your arm straight above your head. Turn the wrist over and now point the seam in the direction of the slips. If the ball is now bowled, the wrist is flicked towards the slips keeping the back of the hand uppermost. You will then get a *leg break*. Now for the top spinner. Right arm straight above your head, holding the ball in exactly the same manner, and wrist bent. Turn the arm slightly until the seam of the ball points straight down the wicket. Bowl the ball, flicking wrist straight and letting the arm follow through straight, and if you have done this correctly you will have bowled a *top spinner*.

Let us return to the arm held straight above the head, with the ball held correctly and wrist bent. Turn the arm until the seam of the ball points to fine leg. For the *googly*, bowl the ball with the arm turned in this direction; flick the wrist, and the ball will go up over the third finger spinning in the direction of fine leg. It should only be a matter of turning your arm and then bowling in that position and you should have little trouble knowing which way the ball is spinning. You will notice I said *spinning* and not *turning*, because on some pitches on which I have bowled it has been almost impossible even to make the ball deviate. If you find that you can only bowl a googly, it is because you have turned your arm too much. I have tried to make this type of bowling sound simple. Actually, spinning the ball is not too difficult, but keeping a length with direction is (or at least I have found it) a continual source of embarrassment.

Left-Arm Bowling

The left-arm bowler naturally aims the ball into the batsman, particularly if he bowls round the wicket. It is not necessary to restrict the bowler to bowling either side of the wicket, except in the case of the slow left arm orthodox leg spin, when it is generally beneficial to bowl round the wicket. The fast bowler who bowls over the wicket tries to move the ball away from the batsman, as well as occasionally trying to swing one in. Left-arm bowlers have one definite advantage over right arm: they are able to move the ball away from a right-hand batsman much more easily. The natural movement of the left arm allows the bowler to cut the ball away, in a similar way to the right-arm off-spin bowler who brings the ball back. All that has been said about the ' *action* ' for the right-arm bowler applies to the left-arm bowler – in reverse, of course.

The fast, medium or even slow googly bowler can use either side of the wicket, providing he alters his field accordingly. The left-arm slow orthodox leg spinner (who spins the ball in a similar manner to the right-arm off spinner) generally bowls round the wicket, particularly when it is wet and sticky. However, on a very true and hard pitch, especially when one has had very little success bowling round the wicket, it is often worth while trying a change of direction by bowling over the wicket.

The left-arm googly bowler comes into the same category as the right-arm leg break bowler, although the stock ball is one that turns in the opposite direction.

The Grip The grip for the left-arm slow leg break is very similar to that of the right-arm off spinner. The index finger is dug into the side of the seam, with the second finger on the seam but far enough away to give purchase to the first finger. The other two fingers lie naturally under the ball. As the arm comes over to deliver the ball, the wrist is cocked and the palm of the hand will now be facing uppermost; the ball is then spun by turning the hand 180 degrees in a forward and downward motion. The thumb has turned from pointing to the on side to the off side during the movement of spinning the ball, and the palm of the hand will still be facing uppermost.

A very useful surprise ball to bowl with the leg spinner is the in swinger. As the left-arm bowler has a tendency to bowl into the batsman, he will not find great difficulty in doing this, especially if the grip and method already described for the right-arm swing bowler are used.

Off and Away Cutters

To cut the ball in or away, whether it be for left arm or right, is virtually the same technique, the only difference being that it is much easier for the left-arm bowler to cut the ball away from the right-handed batsman. The reason for this is that the left arm naturally turns over in this direction.

The grip for the off cutter (right hand) is as follows: the ball is held with the seam pointing in the direction of fine leg, the first two fingers held almost together and placed diagonally across the seam, with the fingertips dug in behind the seam on the off side. On delivery the wrist is cocked, and as the ball is bowled the straight fingers cut down across it in a clockwise direction. The action can help in this delivery, as the ball is brought down with the arm and body behind it. The right hand should finish the delivery by going well past the left side. This is not a particularly difficult ball to bowl, although one must not expect the ball to move very much. Obviously the faster you bowl the ball, the less you must expect it to move.

For the leg cutter the ball can be gripped in a similar manner except that the seam now points to slip and the last joint of the two fingers is now placed facing the on side. When bowling the

Figure 32 Grip for the leg cutter

off cutter, the palm of the hand should face the off side, but for the leg cutter the palm will face the leg side. I need hardly say that the leg cutter is a much more difficult ball to bowl, as the arm is moved in an unnatural direction. On a pitch which gives some help, a good bowler who can cut the ball can be very difficult to score off, as he is able to be so much more accurate than the finger and wrist spinner.

Throughout this book I have described the various grips for spinning, swinging and cutting the ball in the accepted orthodox ways. These grips are probably the best way for the beginner, but if you can already spin the ball or make it swing more successfully in any other way, it would certainly not be advisable to change. Tich Freeman held the ball between his first two fingers; he did not use the third finger for spinning, although it is the one most used by orthodox leg-break bowlers. (He managed to get 300 wickets in one season!) If you are not getting wickets, perhaps a more orthodox grip would help. Unfortunately it is not just the grip that matters; it is the implementation of run-up, action and follow through, coupled with correct technique.

Bowling Leg Breaks

Bowling leg breaks is enjoyable, heartbreaking, back-breaking and exhilarating, very frustrating and very satisfying, but one thing it is not, and that is mechanical. I remember a well known member of the Press asking me, ' Why don't you have two short legs when you start bowling?' The answer is that if I were a machine and only needed switching on, and the ball dropped on a length, I probably would, but being a leg-break bowler and likely to bowl short, I have some thought for the poor fellow who has to crouch in fear at short leg.

The off-break bowler and the left-arm orthodox bowler are much more mechanical than either the right-arm leg break or the left-arm googly bowler, as the method of spinning the ball is much more natural. There is also not quite so much wrist used, and in consequence the ball is not spun so much. One expects this type of bowler to be much more accurate. I think it is a great mistake for any bowler to mix leg breaks and off breaks as, apart from field-setting difficulties, the physical side is so utterly opposed.

The main concern of any bowler is the state of the pitch on which he will have to bowl. How will it react to spin, how quickly will the ball come off, and will it in fact help his type of bowling? The answer to these questions is usually found

F

after a few overs, and the field has then to be set accordingly. One must not of course forget to take into account the technique of the opposing batsmen. Leg-break bowling is an attacking method and therefore an attacking field should be set. The great difficulty is that leg breaks, not being easy to bowl, can be rather expensive, particularly if one uses an attacking field. Obviously this depends a lot on how well one is bowling.

Let us imagine that I am starting to bowl on a fairly fast pitch which will allow the ball to turn a little. If things are going well for me, I will probably try to set an attacking field, with a slip, a gully or short third man, cover, short extra, deep mid off and mid on; a short leg in front and one behind fairly fine, and perhaps one square, all in a catching position. Bowling at my pace, the normal bad ball is short, and this can be either square cut or hooked. In the case of bowling too many short balls, the short third man or gully would go deep and square,

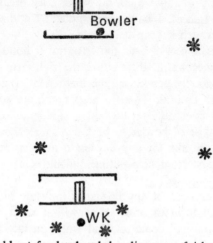

Figure 33 Field set for leg break bowling on a fairly fast pitch

and one of the short legs would drop back on to the square-leg boundary slightly behind square. I would try to pitch the leg break on the middle and leg stump, and make the batsman play forward. If I could keep the ball pitching accurately, I found that it was possible to do without an extra cover and this would allow me to have either an extra slip or short leg.

Occasionally I would try to pitch a googly on the leg stump in the hope of inducing an 'inside edge' to one of the short legs. If a batsman could spot the googly it was, of course, not much use bowling too many on the leg stump, just an occasional one to keep him thinking. In this case, I had to do without the short legs and bowl more towards the middle and off and bring back my extra cover. I did bowl a fast ball without spin as a surprise ball, and providing I managed to bowl it straight, it did get a few wickets. I had to make a sign to let Godfrey Evans know when it was coming, not for Godfrey's benefit, but in order that he might warn the slips as discreetly as possible. If I managed to get a leg break or a googly past the bat, I would often bowl a quick one next ball, but to become too stereotyped was a bad thing, as batsmen soon noticed what was happening. I do admit to bowling a googly first ball to most batsmen, as although I knew they expected it, they could not be sure. However, it is not a bad idea to let the batsman know exactly what you bowl and then let him guess what the next delivery will be.

One of the most difficult wickets for a leg-break bowler to bowl on is the sticky pitch where the ball turns a lot. Because the ball turns, you must pitch it up nearer to the batsman, and you must make him play forward. Your margin of error is diminished considerably and you also have to push the ball through much more quickly to make it *hit* the ground. The googly is of little use on a wicket like this and need hardly be used. You must try to pitch the ball up on the leg stump, but if you occasionally bowl the short ball you must place your square leg deep, and in this case in front of square. You will note that on the faster pitch the square leg was placed behind square.

Whenever you get a new batsman, and whatever the state of the wicket, try to attack him immediately and keep him facing the bowler as long as possible. It is amazing how quickly a fielding side revives after a success or two and fresh batsmen become at least a little apprehensive.

I have never been in favour of bowling leg breaks from well behind the crease, or of using the width of the crease as seam bowlers often do. I found it difficult enough just trying to spin the ball and keep it on a length, and I would advise any young bowler not to try to do too much, as there is plenty of natural variation in this type of bowling.

Godfrey Evans was never in any trouble with the googly. I also had a very good idea of those batsmen who could see the googly and those who were not quite sure. It did not necessarily mean that one got the wicket of a batsman who was in doubt about the googly, as one had to pitch it in the right spot and either hit the pad or the wicket.

Talking of batsmen who could see the googly: Kent were playing Notts at Gillingham, and I was bowling the last few overs of the day against the Notts opening pair. Kent had batted all day and declared, leaving Notts about half an hour's batting. The batsman concerned was Charlie Harris, and I knew that he was one of those who was in no doubt about seeing the googly. (By the way, he was the leading comedian in county cricket at that time.) Whenever I bowled a googly to Charlie he would shout down the pitch, well before the ball had reached him, 'Googly, Doug!', and I must admit he was never wrong. As the day was nearing its end Notts were not anxious to chance hitting out, but we were very keen to get a wicket. It came to the last over, and with my third ball I once again tried a googly, hoping that it would turn a little more and perhaps get an inside edge. Once again Charlie shouted back, 'Googly, Doug.' However, this time the ball did not turn; it went straight on and hit him on the pad, which appeared to me to be plumb in front of the wicket. I thought it worth an appeal and it was successful. Charlie had to go. Poor Charlie was furious and, to

make matters worse, on his return to the pavilion his bat, somehow or other, broke a window!

On another occasion I was bowling to Arthur Wellard of
Somerset. He could see the googly, and whenever I bowled it
he always tried to hit it for six. Five times I threw up a googly
and five times he tried to hit me for six, and five times he was
dropped on the boundary!

Such players as Compton, Bradman and company did not
concern themselves as to whether or not the ball was a googly;
they played the ball either off the pitch on the back foot or got
to the pitch when playing forward. It really does not matter
how much you spin the ball if the batsman gets to the pitch,
and that is why I have continually stressed this.

Captain and bowler should be constantly on the alert for any
weaknesses that show up in a particular batsman, be ready at
all times to exploit these weaknesses and prepared to adjust
field placings in the hope of taking a wicket. I should perhaps
explain at this stage that the field setting illustrated in figure 33
is *not* an arbitrary one; rather it was one which I found very
effective for my type of bowling under certain conditions.

For the young leg-spin bowler, who is probably best advised
to concentrate his line on the middle and off stumps, a more
conventional field setting is preferable. I suggest slip, short third
man, mid-off (deepish), cover and short extra on the off-side,
with deep mid-on, mid-wicket and backward square leg (both
no deeper than the umpire) and a deep square-leg. If the batsman is especially strong on the off, one of the leg side fielders
can come across to allow the use of a deep extra cover. All close
to the wicket fielders should be positioned to prevent the quick
single.

5
Fielding and Wicket-keeping

You may practise running and throwing, catching and bending from early morn until dark, but you will never be a competent member of a fielding side until everyone in it has decided that *he* is going to concentrate on every ball that is bowled. Every fielder must think and hope that the ball is coming to him, even if he is fielding at fine leg and the ball is going in the opposite direction to the off-side boundary. The ball may be stopped and thrown in, and if you are anywhere in line with the throw, however deep you may be, you should be ready to back up. I am convinced that a fielding side is twenty-five per cent better if it can go into the field with the intention of running for the ball as quickly as possible, throwing each return back into the keeper's hands, backing up whenever possible, and keeping an eye on the captain for minor field adjustments.

Of course there is a technique for fielding, but it requires all your concentration and attention to put it to good purpose. Naturally there will be some who are able to field much better than others; they can run and bend, throw very accurately, and are generally much more athletic. Many soccer players are extremely fine fielders, particularly ground fielders. Then there are those with good eyesight and quickness of reaction, who make fine slips and short-leg catchers. Often the better batsmen make good slip fielders.

Not enough time or thought are given to fielding, to the correct way to hold the hands when going for a high catch, and to accurate throwing. I do not agree with long sessions of fielding practice and would rather see a few minutes devoted to it each day, providing everyone takes it seriously. Colin Bland, the

South African, is obviously very athletic, but he became a quick and accurate thrower only by continual practice. I have seen many fine fielders, such as Learie Constantine, Don Bradman, Cyril Washbrook, Wally Hammond and Clive Lloyd, and they all appeared to be quite confident of their ability. The lesser mortals (and I was certainly one of these) had difficulty in maintaining confidence; if one put an easy catch down, the next catch that came along was even more difficult, and in time one would get to hope that nothing would come your way.

Fine fielders today are Clive Lloyd of Lancashire – a genius in his own right – Mike Denness and Luckhurst of Kent, Greig and Mike Griffith of Sussex, plus Paul Sheahan, the Australian Test player.

To become a competent fielder one should first learn the technique and then practise it daily. In this way one will improve not only one's fielding but also fitness, and gradually gain in the essential confidence.

Defensive Fielding

To stop the ball from a hard drive is defensive fielding; to return it to the wicket-keeper full toss at a smart pace, if the batsman decides to run, is attacking fielding.

Defensive Get in line with ball, keep hands well open and head down. Do not take your eyes from the ball until it is firmly in your hands. The heels should be kept together.

Long Barrier A very sound method of stopping the ball from a particularly hard shot is by turning sideways to the line of the ball and going down on the left knee, so that it touches the heel of the right foot at right angles to the line of the ball. The hands and head must be kept well down; the legs and the body are now right behind the ball, and whatever it does it should at least be stopped by you. From this position you must be quick to gather the ball and get into an attacking position to throw it. These two positions need continual practice; it is necessary not only

Figure 34 Defensive fielding position

Figure 35 Long barrier fielding position

to get into the correct position but also to get there quickly.

Attacking Fielding

The ideal way of fielding, of course, is to attack whenever possible. The better the fielder the more he will try to attack. The technique is to be on the move before the ball is hit and then to anticipate from the shot the direction the ball will take. Having decided the line the ball is taking, try to get to it as quickly as possible. Approach the ball in a sideways manner and pick it up as it reaches the right foot, keeping your head

Figure 36 Attacking fielding position

down. The weight of the body is now on the right foot, and from that position you get into the throwing action very quickly. The left arm and leg are pointed at the target, and the ball is thrown as you transfer the weight from the right leg to a braced left leg.

Catching

The hands pick the ball up, and they catch the ball, and in theory they should always stop the ball. The hands are therefore extremely important, yet many people fail to use their

Figure 37 The throw

hands properly or appear not to know how to hold them for either ground fielding or catching. Spread the fingers out as wide as possible, then with palms uppermost bring the hands together until the little fingers are touching, and then close hands until there is no gap between them. Now make a cup of the hands with the fingers still stretching apart and this will give you the correct position for the hands for ground fielding or catching.

For ground fielding the fingers are pointed downwards and for high catching the fingers are pointed almost vertically. Try to get the hands in this position as soon as possible particularly when taking a high catch. With ground fielding it is more difficult to get the hands in the correct position but try to get your hands ready to receive the ball as you go down. I have often seen a fielder running for a high catch and getting well under the ball, and then at the last moment he claps his hands up on to the ball. When you are under the ball, get your hands ready, and then you will not jerk at the ball but let it sink into your hands which, for a high catch, should be just above eye level, and then let the hands give slightly as the ball is caught.

Figure 38 Hands cupped for catch

For the slip catch and for short legs, the technique of catching the ball is exactly the same. The hands are held in the correct position as the bowler is running up to bowl. All fielders except first slip and wicket-keeper should watch the batsman. First slip and wicket-keeper watch the *ball* all the time. There are times when it is not possible to use both hands for a catch, and it is very difficult when one is running full tilt to position the hands correctly.

Brian Luckhurst of Kent is an extremely fine fielder who always looks as if he is going to catch the ball, because he gets into the correct position very quickly and takes time to poise himself to make the catch. A high catch should be taken about chin high; this will allow you to keep your eyes on the ball the whole time, and as the ball enters the hands they can give slightly. This 'giving' with the ball must not be overdone, although it is helpful in absorbing the force of the ball. To push the hands towards the ball is wrong and is often the result of not getting the hands into position early enough.

Field Positionings

It is quite useless putting on the boundary someone who can

neither run nor throw, and you must keep your specialist slip and short leg in their correct positions. It therefore often falls to the lot of a bowler to spend some time in the deep. I would rather go to the deep to field even when I was bowling, as I found that I could get a few minutes to reflect on my bowling and on what I should do during the next over. At least I could run and throw, and I certainly was not missed in the slips!

Even if one is fielding well away from the bat one must always concentrate on moving in when the bowler runs up, and making sure that you are backing up. Never stand so far away that the batsman can run two runs, as nothing upsets a bowler more than a batsman getting two runs off the edge because third man is asleep. If it is a fairly short boundary you will obviously stay as close to the line as possible, but on some grounds, when the wicket is pitched at the opposite side of the square, it may be an extremely long boundary, and in this case it is better to field in a position to allow only one run. It is often better to stand ten yards in from the boundary, particularly when fielding in front of the wicket, as this will allow you to run either ten yards forward or back, thus covering twenty yards, but if you stand on the boundary you will be able to cover only ten yards forward. Most fast bowlers are generally strong throwers, but care should be taken that a bowler does not 'throw his arm out' from the boundary.

For cover and extra cover, mid off and mid on, all should move back before the bowler runs up, come in slowly with the run, and be on the move as the batsman plays his shot. Anticipate the direction of the ball, and then get to it as quickly as possible. Always be ready to go to the wicket if the bowler cannot get there, or to back up – but not too close to the stumps.

There is sometimes a little confusion among slip fielders as to how deep they should stand, and also how far apart. The distance they should stand from the bat is obviously determined by the speed of the bowler and the pace and state of the pitch. If the bowler is not known, then trial and error will have to be used to get the correct distance. If the bowler is fast and the wicket-keeper stands back, one can much more easily find the correct position as the 'keeper will station himself to receive the ball comfortably about waist high, and slips should be about a yard behind him. The distance they stand apart is measured by stretching the arms sideways at shoulder height and then leaving about a foot between the outstretched hands. First slip should be careful not to stand too straight or he may find the 'keeper getting in his line of vision. It helps to have an understanding between 'keeper and first slip as to the distance each will cover.

It is sometimes rather difficult to know exactly where gully should stand. If the bowler keeps a length, then there is little difficulty, as gully can come in for the catch off the edge, but he cannot be expected to catch the ball slashed off a long hop. A good gully must be a very courageous man, and I must put in this class those who field at short leg, because they rely so much on the accuracy of the bowler.

Wicket-keeping

Having spent all my cricketing life with a wicket-keeper of top grade, I suppose I am perhaps too critical of anyone who falls even slightly below his extremely high standard. When I first came to the Kent side, Leslie Ames was the first choice for England, and when he was playing in Test matches, Kent could call upon another wicket-keeper in the same class – W. H. V. Levett. Leslie Ames was a very fine keeper, not an acrobat as another great Kent keeper, but very sound and quietly competent. Apart from his keeping he was, of course, a batsman of the highest calibre. I do not wish to pass over Leslie Ames's keeping too lightly; he was so efficient that he made things look almost too easy – and records speak for themselves. W. H. V. (Hopper) Levett, who went to India with the MCC, was a wicket-keeper of the highest order who, on his day, was probably as good as anyone before or after his time. His keenness and complete dedication to wicket-keeping and his limitless courage emphasized the qualifications so necessary to a good 'keeper. He was not just a good 'keeper – he was a great one.

One would have thought that it would have been impossible to follow these two great 'keepers, and yet Kent produced yet another wicket-keeper of world class in Godfrey Evans. I suppose that Godfrey's best performances have never been surpassed. He was quick, strong, completely fearless. He could always rise to the occasion, and his greatest moments were in Test matches. In 1946, when he really made his mark, he kept superbly in Australia – during one game a thousand runs were scored without a single bye.

What a wicket-keeping treat it was at that time, as Australia had Don Tallon who was magnificent behind the stumps. Each in his own way, these three Kent wicket-keepers influenced the fielding side to greater efforts. As a bowler, one knew that even 'half a chance' became a possible, and even a bad return was gathered so well and quickly that it looked almost good. To have complete confidence in one's keeper was very reassuring to say the least, and the dynamic character of Godfrey Evans and the enthusiasm and happy-go-lucky approach of Hopper Levett were extras which few sides could match. If you can find a wicket-keeper who is sound, and also has unbounding energy, tremendous courage and a sense of humour, you are indeed a lucky side, as lucky, in fact, as Kent have been these past few decades.

Who would have thought that after these three yet another one would come, who in every way measures up to his illustrious predecessors? Alan Knott is a wicket-keeper as sound and brilliant as any. It is interesting to know that Alan Knott was not influenced by T. G. Evans – in fact he says that he did not see Godfrey keep until he came on to the Kent staff. This is quite remarkable, as their methods are so much alike – both are extremely quick in moving behind the ball. Knott is an outstanding example of activity combined with concentration, as his many great deeds for the current England side have proved so often. He is a study in alertness, and his enthusiasm for every ball bowled communicates itself to all his colleagues. Have you ever seen him still for a second during a TV Test match broadcast? I certainly haven't.

The technique of wicket-keeping has not changed recently, although the emphasis is now on getting right behind the ball by moving both feet. All the 'keepers mentioned here have used this method, and therefore fitness is an essential part of training. I know that both Evans and Knott have spent many hours training. Having watched Godfrey Evans for the greater part of his career, and as his method is accepted by everyone to be very sound, I will confine myself to him, and refer to his hints. However, I am sure that the remarks would be confirmed by all good 'keepers.

There are certain fundamental principles which are absolutely essential to success. As each facet of the game is mentioned, so these words are repeated. Batting, bowling or fielding – there is a 'technique' for everything; or there is a method which, if used by most people, will give the best results, I think that I would say that unless these fundamental principles are used to some degree, failure is very probable. For the average cricketer it is imperative to stick as close as possible to these principles, and I think you will find that the great players have automatically used correct methods. This may possibly cause some comment, but all the great players whom I have met can and do play very correctly when necessary.

Preliminary Position, Stance. The wicket-keeper should position himself so that:
1 He is comfortable and without strain
2 He can get a good sight of the ball
3 He can take the ball easily
4 When standing up he can touch the stumps without too much reaching

Position A wicket-keeper must stand either right up or back; there is no half way. The wicket-keeper and the bowler should talk things over regarding methods of bowling and try to

Figure 39 Wicket-keeper's stance

establish an understanding. Some medium-pace bowlers like to have the keeper standing close up while others prefer to have him standing back. Alec Bedser always wanted Godfrey Evans to stand up as he said that it helped him to visualize the good length and gave him confidence. Shackleton of Hampshire, who bowled the same pace as Bedser, was more happy when the 'keeper stood back. There are also personal idiosyncrasies of the 'keeper who feels he is more likely to catch the ball when standing back, than up at the wicket. Other 'keepers feel that perhaps they could get a good stumping on the leg side. All these things should be considered by wicket-keeper and bowler.

It is very important that the wicket-keeper stays down as long as possible (figure 39), only rising to meet the rise of the ball off the pitch (figure 40). His body should be behind the ball whenever possible, with the fingers pointing down.

For taking a ball on the off side, the wicket-keeper should try to take the ball into the left part of the two hands; in this way he will ensure getting right behind the ball. For the leg side, try to take the ball in the right hand. Give a little with each ball and go through the motion of breaking the wicket fairly often, and always if the batsman is forward. More important points to watch in wicket-keeping are:

1 Watch the ball from the time the bowler starts his run
2 Make sure you get a good view of the delivery of the ball (you may have to stand a little wide of the wicket)
3 Be balanced on both feet so that you can move either way very quickly
4 Get your body well behind the ball, except when you think you have a chance of stumping off a wide ball
5 Do not ' snatch ' at the ball; let it sink into the gloves and try to ' give ' with it

The wicket-keeper must concentrate on each ball and, if standing back, must be up to the wicket in a flash. He must be ready for short runs, quick returns from fielders, and any extremely high and difficult catch near the wicket. He can also be invaluable in appeals for lbw.

Equipment It is essential that the wicket-keeping gauntlets and the inner gloves are of good quality. They should have as much protection as possible without being too stiff and awkward, and should feel very comfortable. It may take a little time to break in the gloves and to mould the hands to them, but once this is done the keeper should feel completely confident with them. The gloves and hands are vital, and care should be taken of the top joints of the fingers; some keepers bind them with tape. In these days of the rubber pimples on the palms it is not necessary to use a dressing, but this rubber will peel off very easily and should be stuck back immediately. The abdominal protector for the wicket-keeper is just as necessary as it is for the batsman, and for the same reason, and anyone who does not wear one should be made to look after himself!

Although the 'keeper does wear pads, they are not for use but only for an emergency. *Never* buy those awful large cumbersome pads made for wicket-keepers only; these should be worn

G

Figure 40 Wicket-keeper balanced, taking a rising ball

only by the very bad 'keeper who has no confidence in his hands or in the accuracy of his bowlers or the fielders. The pads used for batting can, and should, be used for wicket-keeping as they are reasonably light and allow the 'keeper to move. What we want is a 'keeper who can move quickly – not one just stuck behind the stumps. Keep your boots well studded and free from too much dirt, or you may miss a leg-side stumping through slipping. *Do not keep wicket in practice nets.* If this advice is adhered to it will save a lot of trouble.

The wicket-keeper should practise catching very high catches, as he is often called on when the catch is close to the wicket. I have seen Godfrey Evans dive to the popping crease to take a catch off the batsman's glove; I have also seen him run from standing back to a position past the square-leg umpire and catch a skier. One particular catch he missed was, I well remember, at Canterbury. There was almost a gale blowing, and Fred Ridgway was bowling with it behind him. The batsman went to hook and got a thick top edge which sent the ball straight up in the middle of the pitch. Godfrey, who was standing back, decided that this was his catch. He moved down towards the ball and when he had got as far as the stumps, the ball was at its zenith. The wind now began to get hold of the ball and it began to drift over Godfrey's head. He immediately back-pedalled, the ball continued to drift, until Godfrey was running backwards, with the ball gaining on him all the time. Eventually the ball won the day quite easily, dropping yards behind him, and leaving the Kent wicket-keeper in a most unusual position of not even getting a touch to the ball.

And now, just to confirm that high-catching practice is necessary, here is another true story of the predicament one can find oneself in when keeping wicket. Kent were playing Middlesex at Lord's. Kent were fielding and the batsman concerned was Jim Smith, the giant fast bowler who had the reputation of big hitting. Leslie Todd, the medium-fast bowler, was bowling, and big Jim hit a good-length delivery straight up in the middle of the pitch. 'Toddy', who had had no luck and a few chances missed, decided to catch this one himself. He started to move down the pitch to get under the ball, then saw how high it had gone, had second thoughts, and decided that perhaps it was a catch for the wicket-keeper. The Kent 'keeper was W. H. V. Levett who on hearing the cry ' Yours, Hopper!' awoke with a start to find himself searching the sky for a ball he could not see. He mentioned this fact to all and sundry at Lord's, prefixing the word ball by an adjective that perhaps we must forgive him using in the circumstances. His cap fell off, but this was to be expected because the ball was by now very high. On trying to get under the ball he had to pass the wicket, but unfortunately he walked straight into and through it, laying the stumps flat. Have you ever tried to catch a very high ball and noticed how it seems to move round and round? This was no exception, and as the ball up above went round and round, so did our wicket-keeper. Once again he was unlucky, as the straps on his pads got entangled, and the more he followed the ball round the tighter his pads became. Eventually he fell and sat in the middle of the pitch. The ball was now on the way down. I was fielding at short leg (probably nearer than anyone else to the catch) and had a good view of the ball; I could see that if Hopper did not move and no one else intervened to take the catch (which seemed extremely unlikely as it never occurred to me that I should do anything) the ball would drop extremely close to where our wicket-keeper was sitting. During this time Hopper had thrown off his gloves to enable him to untangle the straps on his pads. At last the ball landed with a terrific smack no more than a yard from the 'keeper. No one else had moved, not even the batsmen; everybody seemed mesmerized by the strange antics of the wicket-keeper, or perhaps they were engrossed in determining the odds on the ball making a hit on coming down. Suddenly the batsmen realized that the shot was at least worth one run, and off they went. Hopper managed to reach the ball and in one movement hurled it at the near end, but unfortunately the stumps lay on the ground and one run was easily taken.

I have seen other high catches dropped by wicket-keepers since that day, but I still have never seen a wicket-keeper practising high catching!

6
Coaching

As a coach I have often been called upon to take a boy or young man whom I have never seen play cricket before. If the person has some obvious ability and has had coaching, it is not too difficult a task. When you meet an advanced player it is often only necessary to correct a few minor faults, and during the time that you are bowling at them you will make a mental note of their attitude to the game. After half an hour's net I think one should know quite a lot about the pupil. A player of some standing has probably explored all the avenues of his ability to find out the best way to play.

For the comparative beginner it is not quite so easy. A young player often has no idea of his own capabilities. Firstly, one must find out what he wants to do, which may not be quite what his natural ability will allow. Secondly, we must find out just how much natural ability he has and in which direction it lies, such as batting or bowling or even both. If his forte is bowling then we have to decide on his action. Has he a good action – fast, medium or slow? If fast or medium, can he swing the ball or cut it? If slow – can he spin the ball, off-spin or leg breaks?

The answers to these questions may be very interesting or extremely dull. The coach must find out exactly what the boy does best (that is, naturally) and try to persuade him to concentrate on this. *Never* try to make a pupil do what you would like him to do, but what you know he is most suited to.

Batting

Although it is best to allow the pupil to have at least five or six minutes batting before making any real assessment of his ability, any very obvious faults should be put right immediately. I have often found that apart from small errors in stance, grip and pick-up, one of the main faults is that many boys do not really know when to play back or forward. This may sound a very elementary fault, but it is a very common one, and I am sure that, if this is so, this is the first thing to tackle. If you can mark on the pitch a line showing the batsman where the ball should pitch for him to play forward or back, and then tell the pupil which ball you are going to bowl, he should soon be able to determine the correct shot for himself. During this time, however, you must also insist that the batsman plays the respective shot correctly, and in this way you will also improve his shot making.

As the pupil progresses, you can put right any minor details (one at a time) which you think will benefit his batting and also tackle the attacking shots. Once you have got the basic shots correct, you should not have too much trouble with any of the others. As I have so often said in this book, these strokes get you into the position for nearly all the other cricketing shots.

Bowling

For the bowler whom you have never seen, allow him to bowl for several minutes and during this time concentrate on watching his action. Never mind what he is bowling or where the ball goes; just watch how he approaches the wicket, his action and follow through. This will certainly give you a very good idea of how he will eventually bowl. Next find out what he is trying to do and how he is doing it. In most cases I think that one will be slightly disappointed, or perhaps, shall I say, not surprised, as it is not often that one meets a boy with a nice easy action. However, one must make the most of one's ability. To alter the action is not an easy matter, but there are certain points which do help and, depending on the boy's determination, surprising results can sometimes be obtained.

What does one look for in an action. Firstly there must be rhythm in the run and in the action, that is, turning and jumping on to the right leg with the left arm raised) and the synchronizing of the left leg hitting the ground and the delivery of the ball. All this must be done with the arms and body kept up straight and yet pivoting from the left side facing the batsman, to the right shoulder. This movement should be smooth and flowing, not jerking or jagged. Sometimes one meets a bowler whose run up and action do not please the eye, and yet there is something in his action which seems to work in a crude fashion, and often one is surprised by the speed and nip he can achieve. There have been several bowlers in first-class cricket who have looked all arms and legs and yet have done quite well because their action has moved perfectly at the vital time, on delivery.

To return to our pupil. Apart from the bowler who obviously can really spin the ball, it is a good thing to experiment with swing or cutting the ball until you find the type of bowling best suited to him. The natural finish of the action will help in deciding which way he might best swing the ball. If the bowler finishes his action naturally with his chest facing well to the off side and his right arm by his left leg, then he will probably bowl a better away-swinger than in-swinger.

The natural ability must be found and used, although at times it may take quite a lot of finding; most people can make the ball do something if one experiments long enough. It is far better to do what comes naturally than to waste hours trying to spin a googly. When you are satisfied that you know the ability of your pupil, concentrate on his strong points, and yet all the time try to improve his action. If it is necessary to change the action, it must be done very gradually or the bowler will lose his interest in trying to make the ball do something.

Whether batting or bowling, the main consideration is that the ' basic principles ' are kept to. If anything goes wrong with a cricketer's batting or bowling, you will always find the correct answer here.

Group Coaching

I have mentioned earlier that I am in favour of group coaching, and I would like to elaborate a little more on the methods used. Firstly, let me say it is not only for the beginner, for who has not seen the first-class player play a few imaginary shots just before going in to bat? He does this for two reasons: one is to loosen up the arms and legs; the other is to get the bat in the correct groove. The correct groove is what we want for all young players, and if they can get a good idea of this before they go into a net they will have much more chance of coping. I am quite sure that in many cases, perhaps in most cases, group coaching is essential. It most certainly is at any school, and in fact it would benefit members of most clubs and indeed many county players to run over the basic principles occasionally.

Imagine a boy who knows nothing about batting going into a net for the first time. He cannot hold the bat correctly or stand correctly, and he has no idea of when to go back or forward. The coach will have to spend half his time showing the poor boy these things and probably the other half of his time will be taken throwing balls from halfway down the net trying to hit his bat. If this boy had had some group coaching he would have been taught how to stand, grip the bat, pick the bat up, and at least the forward and back defensive shots. He would have learned the cricketing jargon and know what a good length, half-volley and long hop are.

Group coaching does not stop at making shots without the ball. We continue by using a tennis ball, and in this way give a boy confidence and the knowledge of when and how to go forward and back. I have taken classes in group coaching in many different surroundings. Some have been extremely fine gymnasiums with beautifully polished floors (I am thinking now of some newly built secondary modern and county schools). I have even taken a small class of boys in a room over a public house. I have never, in over twenty years of coaching, had any accident or breakage of any kind. If the cricket shots are played correctly, the beautifully polished floors will come to no harm because, apart from the stance, the bat should never touch the ground.

Let us now take a class of twelve pupils in the basic principles of stance, grip, pick-up, forward and back defensive shots. A short line representing the popping crease should be drawn for each pupil. The coach then explains the stance, grip and pick-up with demonstration. After the coach has finished, the class can be formed into six pairs, and each player instructs his partner until both are satisfied with their performances. The next lesson is the forward defensive shot. This is explained by the coach, and again the class in pairs can instruct and criticize one another. When the coach is satisfied that all pupils can play this shot he may decide that a tennis ball can now be used. A ring is drawn on the floor just in front of the batsman; the ball is thrown under arm from about six or seven yards away (rather depending on the room available) so as to land in the ring, and the batsman plays a forward defensive shot. It is absolutely essential that this shot is played correctly to keep the ball on the floor. The class can be formed into fours, a bowler, batsman and two fielders on each side. Each will take his turn in batting etc., and a further two rings can be marked on the floor, one on the off side and one on the leg side. A tremendous amount of good can be done by continually practising this shot, providing it is done correctly, as it will groove the stroke and allow it to be played automatically.

The next shot, the back defensive, should be demonstrated and then practised by the class in exactly the same manner. When each one is satisfied that he can play this correctly without the ball, a tennis ball can then be used. A mark is made fairly short of the batsman, and the bowler must take care to keep the ball close to this mark; if the ball bounces a little too high he may find that by kneeling down and throwing the ball it will not bounce so high. By trial and error you will find the correct length and the best way to throw the ball. Once again,

I would like to be most emphatic that the ball should be played correctly, that is, defensively, making sure that the batsman gets behind the point at which the ball pitches, providing it pitches in line with the wicket. When this shot can be played correctly by everyone, the next step is to combine the two shots. Mark out the good-length spot for forward shots and a clear indication of when one should play back. To help the beginner at first, it is better to tell the batsman, before the ball is thrown, which shot he should play – forward or back. After a time he can be allowed to decide for himself, and in this way he will gradually appreciate the different techniques. Before any other shots are taught, these two should be thoroughly digested. In the case of very small boys it is better to allow them to hit a few cross-bat shots (make sure they are short and well outside the leg stump) and then imperceptibly to coax them into making straight-bat shots as well.

Unless a boy has a fair knowledge of the basic principles I would not consider him ready to use a net. I really am quite convinced that many boys who are allowed nets at our schools would benefit greatly from several sessions of group coaching. What a waste of time for everyone when the coach is continually running down the net to explain some elementary point, yet how difficult it is to get some cricket masters and pupils to appreciate this fact!

7

Leg Spinners

Ever since I first saw Major G. A. Faulkner bowl in the nets at his indoor school at Walham Green, I have been very interested not only in bowling leg breaks, but in all who bowled leg breaks from all parts of the cricketing world. How did they hold the ball, which finger did they spin it off, how could one tell the googly, how quickly or slowly did they bowl, was it a good action, etc., etc.

The Major, although he was not young and was putting on a little weight, still had a nice easy full action – arm still high and follow through thudding against his back. He told me ' A bowler should have a red patch on his back where his right hand keeps hitting '. The speed he bowled was ideal as it was not too slow to allow a batsman to get down the wicket, yet had enough flight to tempt him. When young he must have been a very fine bowler, and I have no doubt that he was the finest coach I have ever known.

During the decade of 1930 until the war, there were some very fine and interesting leg spinners. For Kent there was C. S. ' Father ' Marriott, a schoolmaster from Dulwich, who came into the side at the beginning of August and always got 40 or 50 wickets. He was a gentle person, with an action like a left-arm spinner – the right arm was swung from behind his back. He didn't wrist spin it so much, but cut across the ball and bowled a very steady length with just enough variation of pace or trajectory. He rarely bowled a bad ball. Bowling at the other end for Kent was A. P. ' Tich ' Freeman. This little man – he was not five feet tall – was like a rubber ball as he bounced up to bowl off a five or six yards' run. He had a superb action with arms high, and he really did spin the leg break and the top spinner. Using only the first two fingers to hold the ball (two very short fingers), he *had* to bowl the ball *up* and therefore got a very round trajectory. He was a very great bowler.

In Australia about this time there was another great spinner, Clarrie Grimmett. I regret that I did not see more of his bowling; I had that privilege on only two occasions. However, even in this short time one could see enough to realize that here was a very interesting although perhaps a little unusual method. His arm was not high, but his rhythm and synchronization were perfect, and he really could spin the ball. He changed his pace and trajectory and kept an immaculate length.

The battle between any great bowler and batsman is extremely interesting. I well remember watching Tich throw the ball up to the new batsman to tempt him to try to hit before he was acclimatized. Against any batsman who could use his feet, Freeman would quicken his pace and bowl at a lower trajectory. To such batsmen (who seem to think that all one had to do to Tich was to walk down the wicket) he would throw the ball higher and he got many wickets in this way. Only the great batsmen can consistently move down the wicket.

Grimmett and Freeman were similar but I think Grimmett bowled a little better to the really great player. However, both were great bowlers.

Two other bowlers similar in method were R. W. V. Robins of Middlesex and T. B. Mitchell of Derbyshire. Both gave the ball air – on their day they were unplayable – but like many leg spinners were not greedy and shared a few runs with the batsman. I remember Leslie Ames making 295 at Folkestone against 'Tommy' Mitchell. On one occasion Les ran down the pitch before Tommy had delivered the ball, and on seeing this Tommy bowled the ball high over Les's head into the wicket-keeper's hands.

About the same time as R. W. V. Robins captained Middle-sex, another leg spinner was whirling them down in the same team – Jim Sims. Jim had a nice high action, very good trajectory and bowled at a very steady pace. His method was orthodox, and on the very good wickets of those days he did tremendous work for Middlesex especially as he often opened the innings as well. One must not forget I. A. R. Peebles (a protégé of Faulkner) who also played for Middlesex; before having trouble with his bowling arm he bowled leg-breaks quite quickly, and I am told bowled superbly on occasions. How lucky Middlesex were in those days with at least four first-class leg spinners!

Each county (except Yorkshire) had a leg spinner in those days: for instance, Peter Smith of Essex, orthodox high arm with nice pace – another product of the Faulkner school; Eric Hollies of Warwick, very steady bowler who spun leg break and googly, taking well over 2,000 wickets, an excellent team man and fellow-traveller. Then there was Roley Jenkins of Worcestershire – who could forget Roley with his almost crab-like run to the wicket? His action was unique and his energy and enthusiasm almost unending. Roley had a wonderful season in South Africa in 1948, bowling extremely well on the hard and fast pitches. Lancashire had ' Wilkie ' (Leonard Wilkinson) who pushed the ball through quite quickly and had surprising pace off the pitch; we went to South Africa together in 1938. F. R. Brown bowled most of his leg breaks for Surrey before he forsook the ' union ' in Australia in 1950/51 to bowl ' seamers ' which he did extremely well. He did, in fact, adapt himself well to the surprisingly damp conditions in Australia during that tour.

Australia has always had someone who could spin a leg break, and in many cases they used a rather lower arm in spinning the ball. Frank Ward came over in 1938, and although his arm was a little low he managed to give the ball air. I am sure this is necessary in Australia on the hard pitches which need the ball ' dropping ' on them and not hitting the pitch. Bruce Dooland, although a good bowler in Australia, bowled extremely well in England during his time with Notts. I believe he used the air a little more in England than he had done in

Australia. This sounds ambiguous but I am sure his technique improved in England with so much cricket. He was easily the finest of the Australian leg breakers, except perhaps for Clarrie Grimmett. Colin McCool was another of the leg-spinners who had perhaps a little lower arm action; he really flipped it. He was also a very good No. 1 batsman – a very useful cricketer.

Richie Benaud and Bobby Simpson managed to get many wickets. I am sorry I was not able to see them bowl more often. Perhaps the most comprehensive bowler I have played against was W. J. O'Reilly. He was not a leg-break bowler, yet he could bowl a very fine leg break. He was not an off-break bowler and yet he could also bowl an off break. For good measure he could bowl a googly, off cutter, leg cutter and away swinger. His aggression, determination and superb control of length make him top of my list of bowlers. John Ikin of Lancashire, who batted so ably left-handed, bowled leg breaks very well in an orthodox manner with his right arm, and even Sir Leonard Hutton bowled quite a well-flighted assortment of spinners.

There were others such as Tom Reddick of Notts, Albert Rhodes of Derby (who could also bowl quite quickly), and C. B. Clarke of the West Indies, and doubtless many more. Why so many leg spinners then and why so few now? I think the answer to this question can be found in the type of pitches prepared. If really first-class, quick pitches were prepared, then I am sure that leg breakers would return.

How does one prepare a first-class pitch? I suppose many people would be very pleased to be able to answer this question. Unfortunately I do not think that many groundsmen are capable of producing the right kind of wicket. If there *are* sufficient knowledgeable groundsmen, then I am very surprised that more first-class wickets have not been prepared. I admit that I do not know how to prepare a wicket, and I only wish that MCC would pay more attention to fostering schemes for helping young groundsmen. The pitch is vitally important and must be kept in first-class condition.

If when the ball pitches, it comes off at an even speed, without stopping or lifting, it will allow the batsman to play at the pitch. Providing he is reasonably close to the ball, he can hit the half-volley with confidence, and keep the ball on the ground. The faster the ball comes off the pitch, the easier it is for the batsman to hit it (if he plays forward at the correct time). The good pitch will obviously affect the degree to which the ball will turn, and the bowler who cuts the ball or spins it very little will find it going straight through, and only those who really spin the ball will be able to move it. However, if the ball does move even a little, it will come off quickly, and this is exactly what the bowler wants. If one bowls a half-volley or long-hop, one must expect to be hit for four. But if one bowls a good length ball which turns a little and nips through quickly, one can have high hopes of a wicket. Runs can be made quite quickly, and wickets can be taken by a bowler who makes the ball 'do' something, and providing the players try to *win* the match, some fine cricket can be played. There is one proviso: a good-paced, first-class pitch *must* be provided.

I have heard far too much nonsense talked of 'scientific field placing'. The bowler can set a field only where the batsman allows – and the major deciding factor of a bowler's penetration is in the pitch. An accurate bowler, such as Hedley Verity or Derek Underwood will always keep runs down, but given just a little help from the pitch they will immediately become wicket takers. There have been very few bowlers of any type who have been able to dominate a game on a really good wicket.

I think that leg-break bowlers have taken more wickets than any other type of bowler, at, I admit, a fairly high cost, but when a batsman has a first-class pitch and a leg-break bowler is on, the cricket is at least interesting with runs coming fairly quickly, yet with an anticipated wicket falling at any minute.

The public want to see the ball hit, and batsmen will not be able to do this satisfactorily until better wickets are produced. When good pitches return, so will the leg-break bowler and, as a matter of course, better cricket. But despite this rather pessimistic note, the leg-spinner is, I feel and profoundly hope, on the way back. Young Warwick Tidy – appropriately of Warwickshire – made a fine debut in 1970 including a splendid performance in, of all things, the Sunday league limited overs match. Robin Hobbs of Essex – a mistakenly selectorial omission from the 1970-1 MCC side in Australia – is always among the wickets as also is jovial Intikhab Alam, the Surrey all-rounder and Pakistan captain.

I think the fault lies not with the leg-spinner but with the lack of courage shown by county captains to use them sufficiently and to 'buy' wickets. Of course, bad wickets produce low scores and if there is one thing a 'leg tweaker' likes it is plenty of runs to bowl at.

There is small doubt in my mind that the eclipse – temporary I hope – of the leg spinner in full employment has contributed to the dullness of modern cricket, especially cricket at county level which is in dire need of brightening up. I trust that captains and committees will do a lot of hard re-thinking on this subject. A good leg spinner will thrive on hard work and his very failing – the tendency for length and flight to stray at times – must produce more stroke invention by batsmen seeking runs.

The failure of England's batsmen in Australia in 1970-1 to 'read' Gleeson's googly and their having to play him 'off the pitch' was to my mind largely due to their lack of experience in playing leg-spin at home.

8

What Makes a Good Captain?

Cricket captains – like all cricketers – come in a vast variety of shapes, skills and techniques, and, like all cricketers again, captains come and go. At international and county level these appointments seem to be particularly vulnerable; they always were, and still are today. In what one might doubly term the 'close season' of 1970-1, captains galore departed either from their counties or from their jobs. It is not my purpose here to go into cricket politics, but it did make me wonder whether all the sackings were based on the inability of the particular player to continue to lead his side.

A good captain does not suddenly produce a superb side from indifferent players; a bad captain does not completely ruin the abilities of the men at his disposal. But a good and successful side is almost invariably well led. However, a side's success does not always imply a great captain, any more than the opposite is true. The better side will win on most occasions; it is only when all things are equal that the really competent captain comes into his own. In my experience – and this probably spans as wide a band of the cricket scene as anyone's – most people who play the game do so to the best of their ability at all times, yet the good captain with the word of encouragement at the right time can get even a little more out of most of us.

At this stage it is possibly pertinent to ask: 'what are the qualities needed in a captain?' You will note that I have not said 'a successful captain', as the first essential is a well-balanced side. Most importantly in my opinion, the captain must be worth his place in the side on his own personal ability and technique. Certain of this and confident that his own perform-

H

ances will be up to scratch, he can then concentrate on the running of the side. And here let me stress that in cricket, as in all other properly played games, the object is to win the match, at the same time observing the Laws and the spirit of cricket. A draw is better than defeat, but the winning side is the happy one.

Obviously a captain must be something of a disciplinarian, but harshness on and off the field does not weld a contented side. My ideal captain would be one who exercised complete self-discipline and by his own conduct led his men by precept and example. This is particularly true at club and school levels where the captain, in his daily routine, is just one of his community. A full knowledge of the Laws and their various changes – plus ' local rules ' are other basic essentials.

It is not given to an otherwise gifted captain to ' read ' a wicket correctly, but if he can do so this is an invaluable asset. But any captain at any level can learn by experience and on one's own ground it is there for the asking – from groundsmen, senior players and so forth. And perhaps here is a good time to stress that the captain who will not deign to seek advice and counsel is making a rod of resentment for his own back.

On the subject of ' reading ' a pitch let me digress a moment for a story about a very fine cricketer and captain from overseas, who had better remain anonymous. Shortly after I retired from first-class cricket I was playing in a charity match in fairly distinguished company. The pitch was particularly green and full of grass – not, in fact, a very helpful pitch on which to stage an exhibition match to which the crowd had come to see sixes hit and strokes played. The great Alec Bedser was in our side and on such a pitch, even bowling at half pace, he was moving the ball off the seam to no small extent and it was difficult for the batsmen to survive, let alone make crowd-pleasing runs. The illustrious batsman said to me at one stage : ' Doug, how you would have liked to have a go on this track a few years ago.' How wrong he was – that particular pitch simply would not take any spin at all, but all a seam bowler had to do was to keep a length and let the pitch do the rest.

But, of course, in my friend's home country they just did not grow grass as green and lush as we do in England and this sort of pitch was completely foreign to his knowledge. It is a rare gift to know your wicket thoroughly, but even those who, by luck or insight, can really tell the good from the bad have often blundered disastrously. But at least on your home ground it is not difficult to find out about the subsoil on which the wicket is laid and to learn reasonably accurately its drying qualities and periods – this is something to start with at any rate.

The duties of a club or school captain start well before the tossing of a coin for choice of innings; in fact, they are never-ending and, all too often, unhonoured and unsung. Possibly the greatest virtue here is sound ' man management '. Get to know your players, not only their cricket abilities but also their pet likes and dislikes, their personal circumstances and their weaknesses.

Team selection becomes very much the captain's responsibility at this level of cricket and I personally am very much in favour of this. It is the captain who has the responsibility of running the side in a match and the choice of who is going to make up the team should be his prerogative. All too unhappily at some levels of the game this is not the case. For a captain to be allowed freedom of choice of his team implies, of course, that he is the sort of man who will put the interests of his team first, last and every time, and that his selection will not be swayed by personal bias against an otherwise suitable player.

A balanced side is the obvious thing to aim at. By this I do not just mean five batsmen, five bowlers and a wicket-keeper – the proportions are probably all right, but in one-day cricket there are many other factors. What, for instance is the good of having five batsmen who can stay at the crease indefinitely and still leave you without sufficient runs on the board when the polite time to declare arrives? What is the use, either, of five bowlers all of whom bowl splendidly in defence and keep down the scoring rate, but are not rapid wicket-takers? The wise club or school captain will aim for balance in his side based on the job that has to be done and look for as perfect a blend of aggression and defence as is available from his resources.

Blended selection of a team too, concerns fielding to a large extent. Given the choice of two batsmen of roughly equal merit, any good captain will opt for the better fieldsman, and the expert close-to-the-wicket fielder is always worth his place. Make this well and truly known to your players – it is often amazing how a man's fielding can improve if he knows that his team place may depend on it. Encourage your players to come to net practice and one excellent scheme for ensuring a keen attendance is to hold your main practice session on selection night. I know of several clubs who do this and, in fact, will not consider a player for the next game unless he has been seen at practice that week – or has notified his captain of the reason for his non-attendance. This need not be an arbitrary rule, but it is a handy tip for cutting out some of 'prima donna-ish' attitudes which the more self-centred players too often adopt.

Remember, too, that your club or school has other teams than the First XI. The good captain will pay almost equal attention to these teams, visit their practices and be always ready with a word of praise for a good performance. Liaise also with the captains of the lesser teams; they can be a most valuable source of information about the merits of up and coming youngsters.

Praise from a captain, if it is to be valued, is not a thing to be bestowed lightly. Be sparing with it, but generous when the accolade is due. It is all too easy to say 'well played' to a bowler who has just taken five wickets and won the match for you, or to the century-maker. But never forget the bowler who has toiled long and hard for no reward, the batsman who has been out of luck, the fieldsman who has been on his toes throughout the innings but has gone catchless. A word or two of sympathy and encouragement can work wonders; your men appreciate your interest in the whole side, they try harder and your reputation is considerably heightened.

Before we discuss captaincy on the field, let me add a few other duties to the over-burdened leader. He should be the first to arrive at a match and the last to leave the ground. He should meet the groundsman well before the start and discuss any problems; if help with the roller is needed he will arrange this. He will be changed well ahead of time and ready to greet the opposition as they arrive; he will also be perfectly turned out – boots whitened, trousers creased, pads spotless – and make sure that his team is similarly immaculate. I have never seen anyone play better cricket for being scruffy. He will contact the opposing captain and agree the hours of play, intervals and so on and also any local rules about boundaries peculiar to the ground. He will also, and this important duty is all too often ignored, make sure that this information has been clearly explained to umpires and scorers; and that the caterers know what are the interval times. These may all seem somewhat trivial to the actual playing of a match, but courtesy is always noticed and your visitors are always glad to be invited to return.

Some fifteen minutes – no less – before the agreed time of start of play your team should be complete and ready to take the field. In the first-class game this is automatic, and failure to start on time carries the appropriate penalty, but I have never been able to understand why club sides who look forward to the match all week are all too often late in starting – why waste a good cricketing afternoon lounging in the pavilion? I heard recently of a practice rigidly enforced in Canada. In the Ottawa League, where the only five teams in the city do battle each Saturday, it is mandatory that both teams are ready to play before the coin is tossed – the side which is incomplete is penalized by the automatic loss of choice of innings. We could apply this in this country to the greater enjoyment of all club cricketers.

I do not intend in any way to give advice to captains on which choice to make if they win the toss – at this distance it would be fatal – for there are so many imponderables, each peculiar to a specific match on a specific ground at a specific time. In one-day cricket the advantages of batting first are nothing like so great as in the county and Test matches, but they are still considerable. On a good pitch the batting captain can to a large extent dictate the course of play, and the timing of his declaration – if any – and the target for the opposition are of his choosing. On the other hand a bad pitch will hardly get much worse in the course of an afternoon's play and there could be some advantage in asking your opponents to bat first.

Most teams have a reasonably static batting order, but there may be occasions when the captain decides to make some alterations. One man may have been short of an innings over the past weeks due to declarations, another may be out of form, quick runs may be needed and the big hitters advanced in the order. These are all part of the batting captain's strategy. What is important is that he explains his tactics to the men concerned so that all understand the reasons and do not feel aggrieved at demotion. The timing of a declaration is another aspect which must be peculiar to each particular match and there are no hard and fast rules – except, as I wrote earlier in this chapter, the object of playing a cricket match is to win it. It is therefore the captain's decision to try to guess how many runs are enough for victory, weighed against the amount of time needed to bowl out the opposition; never an easy decision to make. There is also an unwritten law of one-day cricket that one tries to allow the side batting second a fair division of time available.

On the field a captain has a multiplicity of jobs and duties and really does need eyes in the back of his head. He must watch every ball bowled and every stroke made and, simultaneously, watch the movements of his fielders. And it is not simply a matter of watching; the captain must be always alert for any signs of weaknesses in the batsman's strokes, constantly seeking to take advantage of these while at the same time foiling the scoring strokes, always keeping an eye on the clock, the scoreboard and the weather.

Luckily the bowler is also searching out the batsman's weak points and avoiding his strong ones. The captain should be in constant touch with his bowler, advising and encouraging, and always on the look out for advantageous field changes. It is probably best, therefore, for the captain to field near the bowler, certainly in front of the wicket unless he is a specialist fielder elsewhere. Mid-off is a favourite position for many club captains for this reason; it also allows the wicket-keeper to return the ball to him for onward transmission to the bowler and thus for the chance of a stealthy tactical chat.

While the captain has the absolute right to set his fieldsmen in position, the wise leader usually does this in full consultation with his bowler who knows the type of delivery he is aiming at and where he hopes to pitch the ball. Only when a bowler is really off form in length and direction should the captain suggest different tactics. Most captains also discuss tactics with their wicket-keeper who is perfectly placed to detect batting frailties. A fielding captain must, above all things, be decisive – indecision on his part will quickly spread to the rest of the side.

In disposing his fieldsmen the captain will, of course, make use of specialist qualifications and lucky the leader who has reliable men at slip and short leg to snap up most of the chances. Not only do these men take wickets, their sureness also inspires the bowlers to greater effort and confidence. Equally the captain will choose his out fielders with the same care; it is not much use, obviously, placing a man on the boundary who cannot throw back to the wicket and through whom the batsmen soon realize there are runs every time.

The captain should remember that on a very fast pitch the ball will go ' finer ' off the bat. This will mean third man and fine leg standing finer and that gully and the backward short leg can be moved a few yards closer to the line of the stumps.

It follows from this that on slow pitches these fielders should be moved to squarer positions, and perhaps a yard or two closer to the bat. The gully position is one which needs constant attention as, if the bowler is well on target, gully should be up ready for possible catches; but if short-pitched balls and long hops are being bowled gully moves to a deeper position ready for the slashed catch off a hard hit.

The captain should reach an understanding with his team to deal with a high catch sent mid-way between two of them – the captain, and he alone, will call out which fieldsman is to go for the catch. Collisions on the cricket field can be painful and a bowler's temper is not improved by the sight of two of his colleagues combining to drop a simple catch which, unimpeded, either could have ' swallowed '.

One very important point to remember when you are going to change bowlers is to tell the bowler you are taking off that this is his last over – and let the oncoming man know at least an over in advance that his turn has come. There is nothing more annoying that removing your sweater ready to bowl only to find that someone has taken over at your end. Prior warning is also very helpful to the new bowler as it allows him time to loosen arms and fingers and to prepare himself mentally for the fray. A quiet word of encouragement to the bowler you have taken off will also not go unappreciated.

Try to conserve the energy of your fast bowlers by playing them in the field in positions where they are not likely to have too much running to do. Give your team every possible help on and off the field, but make sure they know that you expect in return a hundred per cent effort at all times and that all instructions be carried out to the letter. Insist on the game being played not only according to the Laws but, what is more important, to the spirit of the game. At the end of a match, if you have been batting second, make sure that your team is on the pavilion to applaud the fielding side. You and your team should also be on hand to make sure that your visitors enjoy whatever hospitality has been arranged; as a matter of common courtesy no member of the home side should leave until the visitors have departed. And do, please, remember to thank umpires and scorers for their services.

One final plea to all captains – encourage your young players, for it is from them that our future cricketers – and captains – will come. Do all you can to run proper coaching sessions for the developing players, and wherever possible see that they are kept informed of, and helped to join, any winter or spring coaching classes that may be organized locally.

9
Case for Non-Turf Pitches

In addition to my coaching duties at Charterhouse School, I have also been fortunate enough to have the chance of passing on my knowledge of this greatest of all games to many other young cricketers through MCC coaching classes at Lord's, at Lilleshall in Shropshire and at the Crystal Palace Sports Centre. I also assisted in coaching classes run under the sponsorship of the Wrigley Cricket Foundation at various centres, including Lord's, and I have visited a great many local authority schools in my part of Kent, plus courses at the University in Canterbury. I catalogue this not boastfully, but to indicate that my knowledge of young cricketers from many walks of life is pretty extensive.

I have always insisted that all coaching be done on good pitches and I feel that this is absolutely essential if a young player is to learn thoroughly the basic skills and techniques of the game, and to have the confidence to apply them in actual play. But it is woefully apparent that some of my young pupils have not before had these advantages and I have seen countless boys, obviously with much good cricket in them, play the most appalling strokes when they have first come to my nets. This can mean one, or both, of two things. The boys have not been properly coached at their schools or they have been given very indifferent pitches on which to practise and play, where the ball pops up hurtfully off a good length and comes through to the bat at a variety of heights. It is, I feel, more than high time that local education authorities looked at this problem of providing proper cricket playing surfaces. I know that groundsmen are hard to find and expensive to employ and that without them the provision of good grass pitches is well nigh impossible. So why not investigate the artificial playing surfaces? There are plenty to choose from and they are not all expensive. I think the results would amply repay the cost.

I have heard it said in Australia that one of the troubles with English cricket is that boys get too much coaching. I do not believe this, but I do believe that one of the reasons Australia can produce so many fine stroke players is because they have so few *bad* grass pitches, but have many baked, almost bare, pitches where the ball comes through at a good pace and at a predictable height. But some of the pitches our boys have to try to play on are so poor that anyone trying to play correctly is in danger of being injured.

I have seen many so-called cricket pitches which have been quite disgraceful and it is disheartening, to say the least, to see boys whom one has coached on perfect indoor artificial pitches trying to cope with these dangerous stretches of grass. Unfortunately on these bad pitches it is the good player who gets behind the line of the ball who is at the greatest disadvantage – and the uncoached batsman, who has little idea of batting but is blessed with a good eye and timing, heaves away to the leg side, often hitting the ball which bounces at a fair height and missing the bouncing ball – off which the better player, playing a correct shot as he thought, is likely to be caught off his glove. To anyone interested in real cricket, please do all you can to improve pitches – and practice pitches are even more important.

The Wrigley Cricket Foundation, which was launched in mid-1969, allocated £50,000 over a five-year period for its aims: ' To stimulate and encourage an interest in the playing of cricket by the young and the achieving by them of a greater proficiency and skill in the game.'

This, of course, means coaching – but coaching itself means so many things if its purpose is to be successful. Firstly the coach has to be skilled and capable of passing on his enthusiasm and knowledge. Secondly the conditions under which the coaching is carried out have to be as near-perfect as possible. Thirdly –

and to my mind the most important factor of all – the playing surface on which the expertly coached boy plays his actual matches has to be true in pitch, bounce and pace.

Luckily the Foundation has as its Secretary Mr J. G. Dunbar, who is also Secretary of the National Cricket Association and an Assistant Secretary of MCC. Jim Dunbar is possibly the most knowledgeable of our cricket administrators in the development of non-turf pitches as replacements for sub-standard grass surfaces. The Foundation has provided funds for research into non-turf pitches in co-operation with the NCA and Mr Dunbar has himself conducted many tests on the numerous materials at present available.

'Basically,' says Mr Dunbar, 'any smooth even surface is preferable to bumpy, rough and badly prepared turf. No boy can be expected – although thousands are – to learn to play strokes correctly if he has no idea what the ball is going to do after pitching. The non-turf surface obviates this. It is an essential for practice and for actual match play, in cases where the original is just not good enough or has deteriorated through lack of maintenance. I am very concerned about the lack of facilities in our schools and I hope that local education authorities will soon begin to take more cognisance of their responsibilities to provide better pitches. We – the Foundation and the NCA – are always ready, and only too willing, to provide advice from the results of our research, and to recommend the type of surface most suited to the particular needs of a ground. But the initiative must come from the authorities.'

In his office at Lord's, Jim Dunbar has an impressive collection of samples of non-turf surfaces, all of which have been tested, and his guidance is there for the asking. The surfaces range from simple coir and sisal matting to the most sophisticated of the man-made grasses now available here and which have been long in use in the United States. This means too a wide variety of cost, so that a non-turf playing surface of one sort or the other should not be out of the reach of any authority that has the initiative and interest in its young people to make enquiries. Cricket started in this country and it should not be allowed to lose the interest of the young simply because it is difficult to find somewhere to play the game properly under good conditions.

It seems to me, too, that coaching standards have gone down rather alarmingly in recent years and I suppose this must largely be due to the many other calls now made on the time of physical education teachers in local authority schools. It was therefore partly with the overworked PE master in mind that this book came into being. I hope it will provide many of them with the sort of guidance which, for one reason or another, they may find a need.